50 STATES
500 DAY HIKES

pil

Publications International, Ltd.

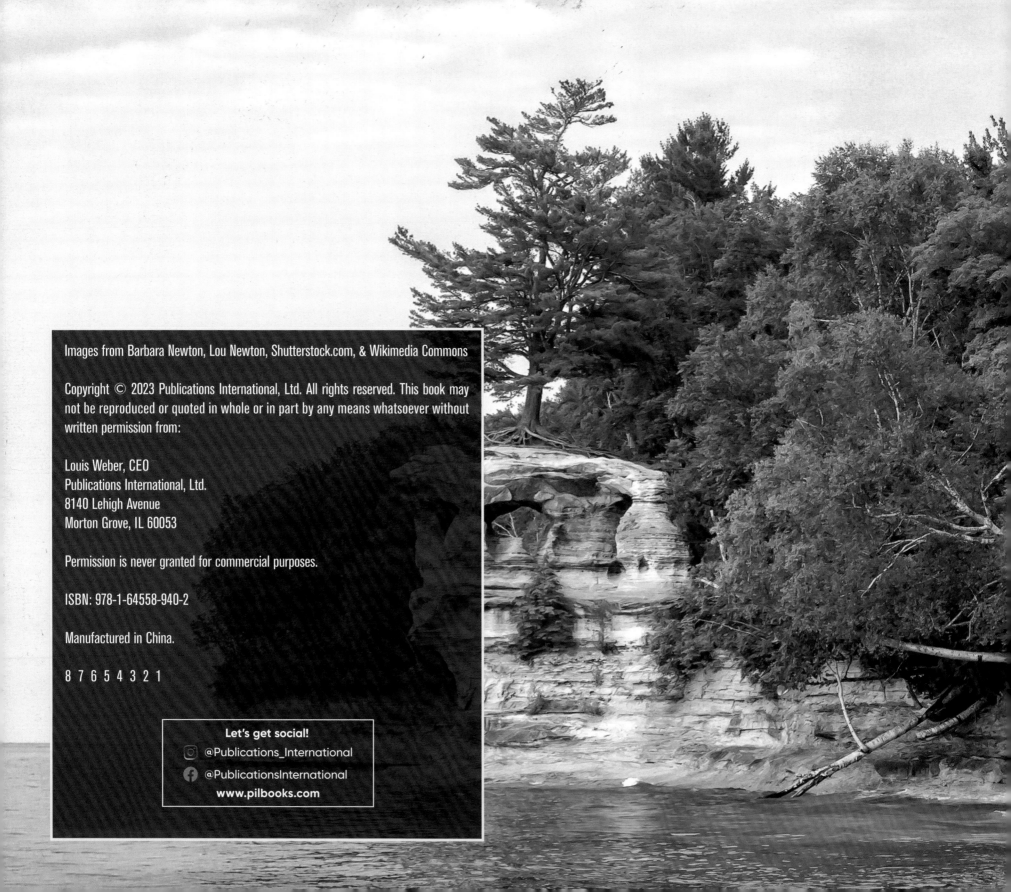

ISBN: 978-1-64558-940-2

Manufactured in China.

8 7 6 5 4 3 2 1

Let's get social!
@Publications_International
@PublicationsInternational
www.pilbooks.com

Table of Contents

INTRODUCTION

Hike along hundreds of miles of trails through the American landscape. See expansive grasslands, long valleys with rivers running down the center, epic peaks, never-ending mountain ranges, and deep shaded canyons. A decision awaits you at every turn, and an adventure awaits at every trailhead. So strap on your hiking boots and go find where you belong.

Hike Old Speck Mountain Trail in Grafton Notch State Park to climb to the summit of Old Speck Mountain, Maine's fifth highest peak. You'll ascend 2,870 feet into the White Mountain's most northeastern range to the top of the range's most northeastern peak in America's most northeastern state.

Below: Looking out across Grafton Notch State Park from near the summit of Old Speck Mountain.

Top: Fifth Falls is the uppermost and last waterfall on the Fifth Falls and Superior Hiking Trail, but it is also the smallest waterfall you'll see that day.

Hike Fifth Falls and Superior Hiking Trail in Gooseberry Falls State Park in Minnesota to travel up the rocky Gooseberry River to its falls. You'll see fabulous rock formations, five waterfalls, and dense northern Minnesota forest.

Hike Overlook Mountain Trail in Overlook Mountain Wild Forest in New York to ascend nearly 1,300 feet into the Catskill Mountains. You'll walk an old gravel road to the top where you can scope the Hudson River Valley below.

Right: A photo of clouds creeping over the Catskill Mountains near Overlook Mountain Wild Forest.

Hike Mammoth Terraces and Upper Ter Loop Trail in Yellowstone National Park in Montana to explore this famous national park and several waterfalls. You'll see the hot springs and magnificent rock formations that are deposited and formed in teraaces before your eyes.

Left: The hot waters from the springs in Yellowstone National Park deposit calcium carbonate and build these terraces over thousands of years.

Hike Hunter Creek Trail in Humboldt-Toiyabe National Forest in Nevada to ascend nearly 1,240 feet to see the thirty-foot waterfall that is at the end of the rocky trail.

Right: Take a second to rest at the end of Hunter Creek Trail and put your feet in the icy water in the pool at the base of the waterfall.

Hike Alkali Flat Trail in White Sands National Park in New Mexico through the exposed sand dunes along the shores of the disappearing Lake Otero. You'll walk up and down the white sand dunes that are not as easy to traverse as you'd think.

Left: A trail marker along the Alkali Flat Trail, which seems to be nearly nonexistent in the shifting dunes.

Alabama

Alabama is America's thirtieth largest state with nearly three percent of its area consisting of waterways. The state has the nation's second largest inland water system. Northern Alabama is somewhat mountainous with the southern section of the Appalachian Mountains terminating in the state. The Talladega Mountains can be found in the East. A great majority of the state is a plain that gently descends as you approach the Mississippi River Valley in the West. Various ecological regions in the area include the Cumberland Plateau, Ridge-and-Valley Appalachia, the Tennessee River Valley, and the Gulf Coastal Plain. The state has one of the highest percentages of biodiversity in America.

Chief Ladiga Trail
Difficulty 2
Hike, bike, or walk this 33-mile paved trail between the Georgia state line and Weaver on Alabama's oldest rail trail. You will see the wetlands, forests, and Talladega Mountains of eastern Alabama as you cross over bridges and restored railroad trestles along the abandoned Southern Railway and Norfolk Southern Railway. Connect with Georgia's Silver Comet Trail at the Georgia state line.

Pinhoti Trail
Difficulty 4
Hike this 339-mile trail that spurs from Georgia's Brenton MacKaye Trail to Flagg Mountain, the Appalachian Mountains southernmost summit.

Pine Beach Trail
Difficulty 2
Hike through the Gulf sands of southern Alabama on this 2-mile trail through Bon Secour National Wildlife Refuge. See the lush, protected wetlands nestled on the shores of the Gulf of Mexico where green, loggerhead, and Kemp's ridley sea turtles all nest.

Alabama Scenic River Trail
Difficulty 5
Paddle down this 630-mile state water trail along the entire state of Alabama through the Tallapoosa, Alabama, and Mobile Rivers. Travel between Leesburg on the Georgia state line to Fort Morgan on the Gulf Coast.

Bon Secour National Wildlife Refuge is one of the largest undeveloped sections of the Alabama coast and serves as a home for several endangered species and migratory birds.

The Gulf State Park was devastated by 2004's Hurricane Ivan, but since then, the park has undergone renovations, including the installation of a 1,540 long fishing pier.

The underground passages of Rickwood Caverns are estimated to be 260 millions years old and have blind cave fish swimming in the underground pools nestled among limestone formations.

Russell Cave was used as a rock shelter several thousand years ago and is considered to be the earliest known settlement in southeast America. It was inhabited from 6500 BCE to 1650 CE.

Little River Canyon National Preserve protects the Little River, America's longest mountaintop river, flowing across the entire length of Lookout Mountain in the Cumberland Plateau.

Lakeview Trail
Difficulty 1
Visit Gulf State Park and hike the 2.2-mile Lakeview Trail around Shelby Lake and then to the beach along the Gulf of Mexico. At Gulf Shore State Park there are several other trails that will show you the shore's rolling sand dunes, pine tree outcroppings, tea-colored streams, and spring-fed lakes.

Fossil Mountain Hiking Trail
Difficulty 3
Visit Rickwood Caverns State Park and hike the limestone mountainside to see several fossil formations in the rock outcroppings beside you. While you are at the state park, be sure to visit and tour the majestic and mystical caverns.

Russell Cave National Monument Trail
Difficulty 1
Hike 1.5 miles into the backcountry of Russell Cave National Monument. While there, take a cave tour of Russell Cave. The cave is Alabama's third-longest mapped cave and was used as a rock shelter for prehistoric peoples from approximately 6500 BCE.

Eberhart Trail
Difficulty 3
Hike just under 1 mile into the Little River Canyon in Little River Canyon National Preserve to visit several popular swimming holes along the Little River.

Chattahoochee Valley Railroad Trail
Difficulty 2
Bike, walk, or run this 7.5-mile rail trail along the abandoned Chattahoochee Valley Railroad through the historic districts of Riverview, Fairfax, Langdale, and Shawmut. Each of these districts were once separate towns connected by the railway, but are now incorporated as the city of Valley, Alabama. See several historic sites along the trail including the Fairfax Railroad Depot and the Horace King Memorial Covered Bridge.

The Horace King Memorial Covered Bridge. Horace King was born into slavery, but after his emancipation, he became a well-known architect who engineered several bridges in the Deep South.

Mountain Laurel Trail
Difficulty 3
Hike 1.4 miles in Cheaha State Park of eastern Alabama to see the Talladega National Forest and Talladega Mountains from the Rock Garden Outlook. Travel through the serene beauty along the streambank under lush hardwood thickets. While at the Cheaha State Park, be sure to visit the several waterfalls that roar in the area.

Sunrise in the Cheaha State Park.

Alaska

Positioned at the northwestern corner of the North American continent, Alaska is one of only two states that is not bordered by another state. Alaska provides more miles of coastline than every other state combined, and is the largest state by area. There are several distinct regions in the state including the populous southcentral Alaska, which is home to Anchorage and several of the state's larger cities, the Alaskan Panhandle in the southeast, the coastal southwest Alaska bordered by the Pacific Ocean and Baltic Sea, and the remote Alaskan Bush and Interior. Nearly sixty-five percent of the state is managed and owned by the U.S. government, which protects the state's deep forests, rugged mountain ranges, glaciers, and pristine waterways.

Tony Knowles Coastal Trail
Difficulty 2

Hike, walk, or bike this city trail that runs 11-miles along the coast of Cook Inlet in Anchorage. In the winter you can use the trail for cross-country skiing. Along the way you will see great views of the city as you pass through several city parks like Elderberry Park, Lyn Ary Park, Earthquake Park. The trail runs between 2nd Avenue in downtown Anchorage to Kincaid Park south of the city.

Top: There aren't many places that can offer views of downtown with such majestic wildlife in the foreground.

Bottom: A view of the Cook Inlet from the Tony Knowles Coastal Trail. The inlet is named after Captain James Cook, who mapped much of America's northwestern coast in the eighteenth century.

Hiker at the edge of Exit Glacier in Kenai Fjords National Park near Seward, Alaska.

Harding Ice Field Trail
Difficulty 5

Hike in Kenai Fjords National Park near Seward to climb nearly 3,812 feet above the treeline into glacial ice fields. Start near sea level in the lush forests and begin your ascent toward the Exit Glacier and Harding Ice Fields.

Flattop Mountain is the most climbed mountain in the state of Alaska.

Flattop Mountain Trail
Difficulty 5

Hike in Chugach State Park just outside of Fort Richardson near Anchorage, Alaska, to the summit of Flattop Mountain. The ascent of nearly 1,400 feet in 3.3 miles quickly leads you to epic views of the park. You'll scramble boulders in the last 500 feet to reach the peak.

The Chugach National Forest is a mountainous region that surrounds the Prince William Sound. It is a temperate rain forest filled with spruce and hemlock trees.

Winner Creek Trail
Difficulty 2

Hike this 4.9-mile trail in Chugach National Forest near Girdwood. Follow Winner Creek through the forest and cross over the Snowcat Bridge before reaching the hidden Winner Creek Falls at the end of the trail.

The Eagle River area is incredibly popular for hiking and over night backpacking in the wilderness.

South Fork Eagle River Trail
Difficulty 4

Hike this 10.7-mile trail near Eagle River in Chugach State Park. While you are in the Alaskan wilderness you will have the opportunity to see otters, beavers, moose, and blue heron. Ascend nearly 1,500 feet as you climb along the Eagle River step-by-bouldery-step.

Along Glacier Lake Trail you'll make your way to Halibut Cove, a small fishing town with a population of 76. Like many coastal towns in Alaska, no roads lead to Halibut Cove, so you must get there by boat, plane, or foot.

Glacier Lake Trail
Difficulty 4
Hike this 10.1-mile trail in Kachemak Bay State Park on the southwest side of the Kenai Penninsula in southern Alaska and ascend nearly 1,382 feet into the alluvial flats where Glacier Lake sits. Meander between old cottonwood and spruce forests toward epic lake views. Take a water taxi back to Homer, if you don't want to hike back out.

The Castner Glacier has an ice cave in which you can explore.

Castner Glacier Trail
Difficulty 3

Hike this short 2.6-mile trail through Castner Creek Canyon up to the Castner Glacier near the town of Fort Greely. Although the trail is not marked well, it follows the creek up the canyon nearly 500 feet. As you get closer, the trail becomes increasingly more difficult with steeper inclines and large boulders in need of scrambling.

The Chitina River flows from the meltwater of the Chitina Glacier and was used as a watershed for the copper miners in the region.

Crystalline Hills Trail
Difficulty 2

Hike 2.8 miles in Wrangell-St. Elias National Park and Preserve near McCarthy through dense forests and along the foothills of the Crystalline Hills. Gain exquisite views of Chitina River, Moose Lake, and the Chugach Mountains.

Hiking through the serene valleys tucked in between the Alaskan Range of Denali National Park. The park is home to America's highest mountain, Mount Denali.

Savage Alpine Trail
Difficulty 4

Hike this relatively short 4.1-mile out-and-back trail in Alaska's Denali National Park and ascend nearly 1,400 feet along the Savage River. Start your hike at the Savage River Campground and find yourself climbing into the serene Alaskan wilderness. The area may be closed at times due to bear sightings.

The Bonanza Mine is a vestige of Alaska frontier and mining history and is a symbol of the determination of humanity despite the rugged hardships nature presents.

Bonanza Mine Trail
Difficulty 5

Hike this 8.3-mile trail only if you are an experienced hiker or adventurer. The Bonanza Mine Trail ascends nearly 4,000 feet into Wrangell-St. Elias National Park and Preserve to the abandoned copper mine on Bonanza Peak high in the Wrangell Mountains. Bonanza Peak housed nearly 5 mines in the early twentieth century.

Arizona

Arizona is the sixth largest state in the U.S. and represents the southwestern corner of the Southwest's Four Corners region. It features several different ecological and geographical zones and is home to several low-elevation deserts, alpine mountain peaks, rock formations, deep canyons, and long valleys. The Sonoran, Mojave, and Chihuahuan Deserts can all be found in the state, with the Sonoran Desert being home to the iconic saguaro cactus. You can also find the Grand Canyon, Monument Valley, and the Painted Desert within this desert state's grand territory.

A patch of prickly pear nestled in the cracks of redbed sandstone. Cathedral Rock, in the background, is a sandstone butte carved by millions of years of erosion.

Cathedral Rock Trail
Difficulty 3

Hike this 1.2-mile trail in the Sedona region to visit the popular Cathedral Rock in northern Arizona's Coconino National Forest. This hike is extremely popular for locals and visitors and can be accessed year round.

The Phoenix Mountain Preserve operates five mountain parks in the Phoenix Metro area, including Camelback Mountain, North Mountain, Papago, Lookout Mountain, and Piestewa Peak.

Fossil Mountain Hiking Trail
Difficulty 4

Hike this 2.1-mile hike through the Phoenix Mountain Preserve to the top of Piestewa Peak in the heart of Phoenix to see sweeping views of the sprawling metro-valley below. This rocky trail climbs nearly 1,200 feet in a preserved pocket of the Sonoran Desert lined with jumping chollas and towering saguaros.

Devil's Bridge looks scarier while approaching it than when you're on top of it taking in the views of Arizona's majestic and mystic red rock country.

Devil's Bridge Trail
Difficulty 3

Hike this 3.9-mile trail through Arizona's red rock territory near Sedona to see a natural sandstone arch in Coconino National Forest. Although this hike is relatively easy at first, the last mile of the trail is steep as you climb the redbed sandstone toward Devil's Bridge.

Flatiron Peak covered in desert wildflowers growing after spring rains.

Siphon Draw Trail
Difficulty 4

Hike to the Flatiron rock formation on this 5.5-mile trail in Tonto National Forest outside of Apache Junction. Ascending nearly 2,200 feet into the Superstition Mountains, you will climb your way to the Flatiron formation. Due to rockslides in recent years, the trail near the summit may be hard to follow, but markers continue to lead the way.

The structures built at Walnut Canyon were constructed by the pre-Columbian Sinagua people, who lived in the region between AD 1100 and 1250.

Fisher Point Walnut Canyon Loop
Difficulty 4

Hike this 10.4-mile trail through Coconino National Forest near Flagstaff to see First Nation cliff dwellings and the unique ecosystems of northern Arizona's shady canyons. You can hike or mountain bike in the area, but please be respectful to the remains of the dwellings tucked into the canyons.

Water features are not Arizona's strong suit, but they are truly gorgeous where they can be found in the state.

Horton Creek Trail
Difficulty 3
Hike this 8.6-mile trail near Payson in Tonto National Forest to follow the quaint mountain streams and creeks through stands of ponderosa pines. You'll ascend nearly 2,300 feet with significant gains toward the end of the trail. The sound of running water accompanies you along your journey until you reach the waterfall at the end.

The lush Coconino Forest is filled with ponderosa pines that surround the foothills of the San Francisco Peaks. Here we see Humphreys Peak emerging between the tree line.

Humphreys Peak
Difficulty 5
Hike to the tallest point in Arizona to the top of Humphreys Peak in Coconino National Forest outside of Flagstaff. This 10.7-mile hike will take you to the top of the state after you ascend the nearly 3,390 feet to get there. On a clear day you can see the Grand Canyon from the top.

Many people say the Birthing Cave is one of Sedona's many healing vortexes.

Birthing Cave Trail
Difficulty 2
Hike this 2-mile hike into Sedona's red rock territory to see the culturally sacred site of the Birthing Cave. The Hopi people in the region used to send their pregnant women to this cave before they were to give birth because of the site's natural powers, and many New Age spiritualists continue the tradition today. Climb into the cave and turn around to see views of the beautiful red desert and rock formations.

The Bright Angel Trail can be extremely difficult at certain times of the year due to rain or snowfall. Rock slides and flash flooding can wash away sections of the trail.

Bright Angel Trail
Difficulty 5
Hike this 15.3-mile out-and-back trail from the South Rim to the banks of the Colorado River at the bottom of the Grand Canyon. This trail is extremely difficult and is recommended for those experienced in hiking and backpacking. Descend and then ascend a total of nearly 4,450 feet to make your way to the bottom of the world's most famous canyon.

Echo Canyon Trail
Difficulty 4
Hike this 2.5-mile trail and ascend nearly 1,500 feet to the top of Camelback Mountain in the Phoenix metro area. Camelback Mountain became a city park in 1968 and offers sweeping views of the entire valley in which the Phoenix metro area is nestled in. The trail offers great hiking and trail running opportunities as well as rock climbing. Along the way, see the Praying Monk rock formation sitting quietly on the camel's back.

Camelback Mountain was named such due to its resemblance to a camel. The "head" of the mountain consists of red sandstone, while the "body" of the mountains is granite.

Arkansas

Arkansas is the twenty-ninth largest state in the United States. Its eastern border is mostly composed of the Mississippi River and much of the eastern part of the state serves as a low-lying delta of fertile grassland. Crowley's Ridge, an ancient outcropping of rock from the Pleistocene that rises about 200 feet above the delta, runs from north to south in the eastern part of the state. The Ozark Mountain Range as well as the Boston Mountains can be found in the northwestern part of the state and offers several opportunities for hiking and mountain biking. In the southeast, pine tree forests tuck away the state's hot springs that were once known nationally for their "healing" properties.

Hawksbill Crag in Upper Buffalo Wilderness. The wilderness was established in 1974 by an act of Congress to protect the headwaters of the Buffalo River and contain sections of second- and third-growth oak and hickory forests.

Whitaker Point Trail
Difficulty 3

Hike this 2.9-mile trail in Upper Buffalo Wilderness near Pettigrew to climb up past waterfalls to Hawksbill Crag. You will only ascend about 500 feet, but the views from the overhang are exhilarating. From there you will hear Whitaker Creek bubbling below you through the valley that stretches as far as you can see.

Hemmed-In Hollow Trail
Difficulty 5

Hike this 5.7-mile trail near Compton in Buffalo National River Wilderness to see one of the state's most stunning waterfalls. Ascend nearly 1,400 feet to the top of the falls, which is the tallest waterfall east of the Rockies and west of the Appalachian Mountains.

A view from the Buffalo River looking up at Big Bluff.

Centerpoint to Goat Trail
Difficulty 4

Hike this 5.9-mile trail in Buffalo National River Wilderness near Ponca in northwest Arkansas. The trail is all downhill on your way in and travels down the bluffs that overlook the Buffalo River. At the end of the trail you'll find Big Bluff, one of the largest bluffs overlooking the Buffalo River. There is also a spur trail at the end named Goat Trail that leads you up a steep 350-foot outcropping with sharp drops on the side.

Be sure to visit Hemmed-In Hollow Falls after a rainfall because the waterfall can dry up.

The Eden Falls Cave has no path inside, but hikers can crawl 200 feet into the cave to explore the large room that features an underground waterfall feeding Eden Falls. Be sure to bring a light because it's dark and be prepared to get muddy and wet.

Lost Valley Trail
Difficulty 2
Hike this 2.1-mile trail in Buffalo National River Wilderness along the banks of Clark Creek and cross several natural bridges along the way. The trail leads to the majestic Eden Falls, which cascades 50 feet into Clarks Creek, and then take a look into the mysterious Eden Falls Cave.

Glory Hole Waterfall Trail
Difficulty 3
This 1.9-mile trail is an out-and-back trail in Ozark National Forest near Deer in northwestern Arkansas. Follow the trail downhill to the falls and be prepared to hike up on your way out. At the end of the trail you'll find the unique waterfall that plummets through a hole rather than over a ledge.

Dismal Creek has carved a hole through the overhang at Glory Hole Falls in Ozark National Forest.

Devil's Den Trail is a moderately easy trail and is great for kids to climb around and explore.

Devil's Den Trail
Difficulty 2
Hike this 1.2-mile trail into the unique rock formations of Devil's Den State Park and explore the many off-trail climbing options it provides for the family. Just outside of West Fork in the Lee Creek Valley of the Boston Mountains, Devil's Den State Park is carved from the sedimentary stone deposits of the Boston Mountains and now features several caves, canyons, and crevices that make this area unique.

A view from atop Yellow Rock in Devil's Den State Park.

Yellow Rock Trail
Difficulty 4
Hike 3.1 miles on this trail through Buffalo National River Wilderness near West Fork and ascend nearly 600 feet to the Yellow Rock Overlook. Looking over the Lee Creek Valley from the overlook, you will see the stunning bluffs and rolling mountainsides of the Boston Mountains.

Lake Catherine State Park is just outside of Hot Springs National Park and was built by the Civilian Conservation Corps in the 1930s.

Falls Branch Trail
Difficulty 3
Hike this 1.7-mile trail and ascend just 200 feet at Lake Catherine State Park near Hot Springs National Park. Walk along the banks of Little Canyon Creek and cross the creek several times before you make your way to the waterfall at the end of the trail.

This moderately easy trail is great for kids to climb around and explore.

Seven Hollows Trail
Difficulty 3
Hike 5 miles on this trial through Petit Jean State Park near Morrilton. You'll walk along a seasonal creek on the wooded path before you come up against large rock bluffs filled with caverns and caves to explore. You see rock formations, and there are even waterfalls depending on the time of year.

Hot Springs National Park is the oldest national park in the system.

Gulpha Gorge Trail
Difficulty 3
Hike this 1.2-mile trail near Hot Springs National Park to connect with several other trails in the national park. You will ascend nearly 400 feet as you climb up out of the gorge and into the rolling hills.

California

California is the third largest state in the United States and is the most populous. Its variety of ecosystems and climates draw tavelers from around the world. From the Sierra Nevada to the Great Valley to the Coastal Ranges and Mojave Desert, California is truly as diverse as it gets. Within its borders you can find the lower 48's tallest point at Mount Whitney as well as the 48's lowest point in Death Valley. It produces all types of agricultural products like avocado, almonds, and pistachios, but it also provides a home to some of the world's oldest, tallest, and largest trees in the world. Enjoy the coasts and its temperate climates or climb extremely tall mountains into treeless alpine regions. The state has something for everyone, and the hikes here cannot be beat.

A photo of Vernal Falls along Mist Trail in Yosemite National Park.

Mist Trail
Difficulty 5
Hike this 7.2-mile trail through Yosemite National Park near Fish Camp to see some of the most exquisite sights America's national parks have to offer. You'll ascend nearly 2,200 feet into the Sierra Nevada Mountains where you'll pass by Vernal Falls, Nevada Falls, and the Emerald Pool.

Potato Chip Rock is a popular tourist attraction just outside of San Diego.

Mt. Woodson Trail
Difficulty 4

Hike this 7.3-mile trail near Poway to climb to Potato Chip Rock and then summit Mt. Woodson in southern California. You'll ascend nearly 2,100 feet into the mountains to see this unique ledge and then gain fabulous views of the Pacific Ocean.

Be sure to hike the Upper Yosemite Falls Trail in the spring to see the waterfall flowing at maximum capacity.

Upper Yosemite Falls Trail
Difficulty 5

Hike this 7.6-mile trail through Yosemite National Park in the Sierra Nevada Mountains to see the stunning Upper Yosemite Falls. You'll climb up nearly 3,200 feet to the top of the nation's tallest waterfall and see the water plumet 2,425 feet to the bottom of the valley.

Built in 1936, the Bridge to Nowhere along the East Fork Trail is as mysterious as the surroundings canyons are grand.

East Fork Trail
Difficulty 3

Hike this 9.5-mile trail in Sheep Mountain Wilderness to the Bridge to Nowhere. You'll ascend nearly 1,200 feet into the San Gabriel Mountains near Azusa and find yourself at an abandoned bridge that crosses the San Gabriel River. There was once a road that led to this bridge, but it was swept away by floods in the 1930s.

Alamere Falls is one of just two "tidefalls" in the state. A tidefall is a waterfall that feeds directly into the ocean.

Alamere Falls via Coast Trail
Difficulty 3

Hike this 11-mile trail in Phillip Burton Wilderness Area near Bolinas to visit the Alamere Falls and the Pacific Coast. The falls drain directly into the ocean, and along the way you will also pass Bass and Pelican Lakes. This wilderness is part of Point Reyes National Seashore in northern California, so be sure to enjoy the quiet and peace along the remote coast.

The mustard plants in full bloom during spring along the Solstice Canyon Loop.

Solstice Canyon Loop
Difficulty 2
Hike this 3-mile trail in Santa Monica Mountains National Recreation Area just outside of Malibu to enjoy everything the coast of Southern California has to offer. Meander your way through this shady canyon and ascend just nearly 700 feet to pass by several ruins of old mansions and also the oldest still-standing stone building in the state. The ocean lies in the distance as you explore the region filled with exotic plants, quaint creeks, and a 30-foot waterfall.

Iron Mountain is managed by the Angeles National Forest. The mountain was once called Sheep Mountain due to the big horn sheep that resided there, but the current name was given to the mountain by the U.S. Geological Survey in the 1890s.

Iron Mountain Trail
Difficulty 3
Hike this 5.2-mile trail and ascend nearly 1,100 feet into the San Gabriel Mountains outside of San Diego. The trail starts with a flat sandy stretch before beginning the ascent into switchbacks up the mountain. Some portions of the trail might be washed away, so sturdy boots are recommended.

Getting to the summit of Mt. Whitney is the accomplishment of a lifetime.

Mount Whitney Trail
Difficulty 5
Hike this 20.9-mile trail to the summit of the lower 48's tallest mountain, Mt. Whitney. Ascend nearly 6,600 feet to the summit to see the sweeping views of the state below you. This trail is only recommended for experienced adventurers because of the extreme challenge it presents.

Eaton Canyon Trail
Difficulty 2
Hike along this 4.4-mile trail through Eaton Canyon Natural Area Park and follow the creek to the waterfall at the end. You will boulder-hop and cross the stream several times in this quiet and shady California canyon.

A photo of Eaton Falls at the end of the Eaton Canyon Trail.

Half Dome rises nearly 8,800 feet above sea level and is the most famous rock formation in Yosemite National Park.

Half Dome Trail
Difficulty 5

Hike 16.3-miles on this extremely difficult hike to the top of the famous Half Dome rock formation in Yosemite National Park. You will ascend nearly 5,300 feet as you hike past Vernal Falls, Nevada Falls, and Liberty Cap to an overlook that gives you views of the High Sierras and the Yosemite Valley below. You'll need a permit to access the trail, but the effort is well worth it.

Colorado

Colorado is the eighth largest state in the United States and represents the northeastern corner of the Southwest's Four Corners region. Colorado's Eastern Plains encompass a considerable portion of the state's eastern side. The Rocky Mountains, North America's largest mountain range, bisect the state from north to south and provide alpine mountains littered with glaciers, lakes, pine forests, whitewater rivers, and snowmelt streams. A majority of the state's population lives in the eastern Front Range Urban Corridor. The Western Slope region of the state consists of high desert plateaus and the rugged San Juan Mountains. The state contains nearly 50 mountains that reach 14,000 feet, so there are plenty of hikes that will provide unprecedented views and challenges.

It is best to hike Emerald Lake Trail between June and October due to the snowy winters, but snowshoeing and cross-country skiing are great options to make the trek in colder months.

Emerald Lake Trail
Difficulty 2

Hike this 3.2-mile trail in the heart of Rocky Mountain National Park just outside of Estes Park in north-central Colorado. You'll ascend just 700 feet into the lush pine forests of the Rockies past three other lakes, including Bear, Nymph, and Dream Lakes, before arriving at Emerald Lake.

Here we see Sky Pond with a granite-spire rock formation, called Skarkstooth, behind it.

Glacier Gorge Trail
Difficulty 5

Hike this 9.4-mile out-and-back trail in Rocky Mountain National Park near Estes Park and ascend nearly 1,800 feet past several alpine lakes to the shores of Sky Pond. Along the way you'll pass Alberta Falls, the Loch Vale, and Timberline Falls, with views of jagged Rocky Mountain peaks that cannot be beat.

A view from atop Black Canyon with the Gunnison River below.

Gunnison Route
Difficulty 5

Hike this 4.3-mile out-and-back trail in Black Canyon of the Gunnison National Park into this terrifically deep canyon. Make your way to the banks of the Gold Medal Water and Wild Trout Water designated river, the Gunnison River, at the bottom of the canyon. Be prepared to ascend nearly 3,000 feet in 3 miles on your way back out.

A view from the Mt. Bierstadt Trail, looking toward Mt. Bierstadt. It's good to leave early on summit trails that are high in elevation due to afternoon thunderstorms.

Mount Bierstadt Trail
Difficulty 5

Hike this 7.8-mile trail in Mount Evans Wilderness near Idaho Springs to complete one of the state's several "14ers." Along the way to the summit of Mount Bierstadt, you'll ascend nearly 2,700 feet through the foothills of Arapaho National Forest, past Scott Gomer Creek, and then up the switchbacks.

A photo of Ute Canyon. The Colorado National Monument is home to many canyons such as this one, whose cliff faces are covered in pictographs from the Ute and Fremont First Nation cultures.

Ute Canyon Trail
Difficulty 4

Hike this 11-mile trail through Colorado National Monument near Redlands. You'll ascend nearly 1,900 feet into the canyon and follow its seasonal stream.

Square Top Mountain is a great habitat for mountain goats, so keep your eyes out for them climbing among the boulders.

Square Top Mountain
Difficulty 5
Hike this 7-mile trail to the summit of Square Top Mountain in Arapaho National Forest near Georgetown. You'll ascend nearly 2,500 feet to the top of this 13,783 foot mountain, just shy of being considered a "14er," but close enough.

The Radium Hot Spring is nestled on the banks of the Colorado River and can be washed out when the water is high.

Radium Hot Springs
Difficulty 2
Hike this 1.4-mile trail near Bond to have a relaxing rest at the end of the trail in the hot springs. A relatively short yet steep climb at the end takes you to the hot springs where the rugged Colorado River is running just feet away.

Not only is the Royal Gorge one of the deepest canyons in Colorado, the gorge is extremely narrow as well, being only 50 feet wide at some points.

Royal Gorge Overlook
Difficulty 2
Hike this 1.5-mile loop trail in Royal Gorge Park near Cañon City to garner views of Royal Gorge. At the bottom of the gorge you will see the powerful Arkansas River.

A photo of the Clear Creek Trail near Golden, Colorado.

Clear Creek Trail
Difficulty 1
Hike, walk, or bike this 20-mile urban trail that connects several cities in the Front Range from Adams City to Arvada to Golden. There are several access points along the trail and much of the trail is paved.

Ancestral Puebloan ruins along the Sand Canyon Trail in Canyons of the Ancients National Monument.

Sand Canyon Trail
Difficulty 4
Hike this 12.4-mile out-and-back trail in Canyons of the Ancients National Monument near Cortez to experience the beautiful landscapes of southwestern First Nation settlements. You'll ascend nearly 2,000 feet and pass several ruins of Ancestral Puebloan structures.

Connecticut

Connecticut is the forty-eighth largest state in the United States and is the twenty-ninth most populous. Connecticut has the highest median income and per capita income in the nation. The south of the state is lined by the Long Island Sound, which provides the state with several harbors and inlets. The coastal lowlands rise into the rolling hills and the low-running Appalachian Mountains in northern Connecticut. The Appalachian Mountains run from south to north in the western portion of the state, continuing on into Massachusetts. The Connecticut River cuts through the center of the state and runs into the Long Island Sound. Many of the state's most populous areas are centered along the Connecticut River Valley.

A stone structure at the top of Bear Mountain.

Bear Mountain Trail
Difficulty 4

Hike this 6.1-mile loop trail to the summit of Bear Mountain in Mount Riga State Park outside of Taconic. Ascend nearly 1,600 feet to the highest peak in the state, but beware of ice on the rock formations during the colder months.

A view from atop Chauncey Peak with the Bradley Hubbard Reservoir below.

Chauncey Peak Trail
Difficulty 2

Hike this 2.2-mile loop trail in Guiffrida Park near Meriden. You can walk, hike, run, or snowshoe depending on the season, but there are a few sections that will require you to scramble up steeper areas.

Ragged Mountain Blue & Red Blazed Loop
Difficulty 3

Hike this 5.6-mile loop trail through Ragged Mountain Memorial Preserve near Berlin into the quiet countryside. This trail is marked with red and blue blazes and is extremely rocky, so keep your eye out for the markers to stay on track.

A view of Hart Pond below the ridge of the Ragged Mountain Trail.

Here we see the ruins of the Roxbury Iron Mines and Furnace Complex, which closed in 1905. The iron ore quarry closed in 1935.

Roxbury Mines
Difficulty 3

Hike this 3.6-mile hike through the woods of Mine Hill Preserve near Roxbury to wander around the remains of an old iron mine and furnace. The terrain can be rocky and the woods can be buggy, so bring your outdoor gear.

Here we see the Comstock Covered Bridge over the Salmon River from the Salmon River Trail. Beware of ticks and bugs during the summer.

Salmon River Trail
Difficulty 3

Hike this 6.5-mile loop trail in Day Pond State Park near North Westchester. The trailhead is located at the Comstock Covered Bridge over the Salmon River, and the trail continues to follow the river and then loops around to Day Pond.

The bridge over Bee Brook at the beginning of the Bee Brook Loop.

Bee Brook Loop
Difficulty 1

Hike, walk, or run this 2.1-mile loop trail through Hidden Valley Preserve near Washington Depot. You'll enjoy the wooded foothills of the Appalachian Mountains and walk on the banks of the Shepaug River.

The Prydden Brook Falls tumbles like a veil of mist down the rocks.

Zoar Trail
Difficulty 4

Hike this 7-mile loop trail in Paugussett State Forest near Stevenson along the shores of Lake Zoar. Ascend nearly 1,000 feet, cross several streams, and see the Prydden Falls as you follow the blue blazes along this trail.

The Sleeping Giant Tower was built in 1936.

Sleeping Giant Tower Trail
Difficulty 2

Hike this 3.1-mile trail in Sleeping Giant State Park near Hamden and climb to the top of Mount Carmel where there is a four-story stone tower. Climb to the top of the tower to observe the surrounding area.

A view of the Wadsworth Falls in Wadsworth State Park.

Wadsworth Falls Trail
Difficulty 2

Hike this 3.6-mile loop trail near Middletown to cross over the shady Wadsworth Brook along two bridges and through the quiet country forest. See Wadsworth Falls as well as the Wadsworth Mansion along the way.

Nestled on an undeveloped peninsula between the Poquonnock River and Mumford Cove on the Long Island Sound, Bluff Point Beach is a great place to find crabs and other crustaceans.

Bluff Point State Park & Coastal Reserve Trail
Difficulty 2

Hike this 3.6-mile loop around Bluff Point Coastal Reserve through the tidal grasslands, salt marshes, and coastal woodlands that are home to several types of seabirds.

Delaware

Delaware is not so large as the forty-ninth largest state in the United States. Such a small area does not leave much room for a variety of ecosystems or regions. Most of the state lies at sea level, and Delaware has the lowest average elevation than any other state. As you move north, the marshy coastal plain rises to the Piedmont Plateau, an elevated region between the Atlantic Coast and the Appalachian Mountains, in the northwestern section of the state. The state's highest point is located at the Ebright Azimuth near Wilmington with an elevation of 447 feet above sea level.

Surf fishing is a popular activity at Henlopen State Park.

Gordon Pond Trail
Difficulty 2

Hike this 6.4-mile out-and-back trail in Henlopen State Park near Lewes. You'll walk along a wooden boardwalk and crushed stone path around the shores of Gordon Pond. At the end of the trail connect to the beach trail and walk back north to Herring Point.

The pine forests found in the Delaware seashore offer unique ecologies that aren't normally associated with ocean-side regions.

Prickly Pear Trail Loop
Difficulty 2

Hike, walk, run, or ride horses along this 3.5-mile loop trail in Delaware Seashore State Park. You'll pass through open meadows and pine and hardwood forests along the shore of Indian River Bay.

A view of the trail in Brandywine Creek State Park.

Brandywine Creek River Loop
Difficulty 3

Hike this 4.8-mile loop trail along Brandywine Creek in Brandywine Creek State Park near Wilmington.

The fall foliage in New England is always a lovely sight.

Alapocas Woods Trail
Difficulty 2

Hike or walk this 1.8-mile trail in Alapocas Woods Park near Rockland. There are several rock walls along the way that are fun for bouldering and "scrambling" up. At the end of the wooded path there is a waterfall and swimming hole.

Rocky Run is a quaint stream that feeds into Brandywine Creek.

White Clay Creek State Park offers 37 miles of trails for hiking and mountain biking.

Rocky Run Loop
Difficulty 3

Hike or run this 3.2-mile loop trail through Brandywine Creek State Park near Wilmington and follow along two creeks, Rocky Run and Hollow Run, through the woods.

Chestnut Hill Trail
Difficulty 3

Hike this 3.3-mile loop trail in White Clay Creek State Park near Newark. Travel between forested rollings hills and grassy meadows.

Drugs are not allowed in Middle Run Valley Park.

Snow Goose Loop
Difficulty 2

Hike this 2.4-mile loop trail in Middle Run Valley Park near Newark. The easy trail is made of wooden boardwalks and crushed stone and provides plenty of shade in the summer months.

A variety of activities are allowed at Lums Pond State Park, including mountain biking and horse riding.

Swamp Forest Trail
Difficulty 3

Hike this 6.8-mile trail in Lums Pond State Park near Kirkwood. Lums Pond was formed as an impoundment of the St. Georges Creek used to reserve water to fill locks along the Chesapeake and Delaware Canal. Hike along its shore and through the swampy woodlands that surround it.

Michael Castle Trail
Difficulty 1

Hike, run, walk, or bike this 12-mile paved trail that follows the Chesapeake and Delaware Canal. The trail intersects with Lums Pond State Park and allows you to explore several other trails along the way.

Northern Delaware Greenway Trail
Difficulty 3

Hike 4 miles between Blue Ball Barn and Brandywine Creek on the Northern Delaware Greenway Trail to see waterfalls and craggy creeks.

Florida

Florida is the twenty-second largest state in the United States. The state is also third largest in terms of its population density with nearly 21 million people in the state. The majority of the state is a peninsula between the Gulf of Mexico and the Atlantic Ocean. The highest point in the state, Britton Hill, is only 345 feet above sea level, and the point is the lowest highest point in the United States. Much of the state is situated on top of limestone bedrock which creates a large system of underwater caves, sinkholes, and springs that provide much of the fresh water to the state's population. Florida is a unique place and offers unique experiences from the swamps of the Everglades to the pine forests of the Panhandle.

A view of the swamps found in Black Bear Wilderness Area.

Black Bear Wilderness Trail
Difficulty 3

Hike this 7.3-mile loop trail in Black Bear Wilderness Area near Sanford. Much of the trail has a boardwalk to keep you out of the muddy wetlands and marshes.

Skyway Trail
Difficulty 2

Hike, run, walk, or bike this paved trail that travels halfway across Tampa Bay along the shoulder of Interstate 275.

Florida Trail
Difficulty 2

Hike, walk, or run along this 5.6-mile trail near Oviedo in central Florida. Walk along the Econlockhatchee River at points, and be sure to watch out for gators creeping on the banks.

A great sunset view of Little Big Econ National Forest.

The Anhinga Trail rises above the mangroves at points with a boardwalk. Be sure to watch for alligators.

Anhinga Trail
Difficulty 1

Hike or walk this 1.5-mile trail through Everglades National Park near Homestead. Along the way you can see a variety of reptiles in the mangroves like alligators, snakes, and turtles.

A variety of flora exists in Florida, and Little Big Econ State Forest is a great representative of that diversity.

Kolokee Loop Trail
Difficulty 2

Hike this 5-mile loop trail through Little Big Econ State Forest near Geneva. The path can be muddy where there are no boardwalks, but this trail has been rated as one of Florida's friendliest trails for families.

The Weedon Island Preserve Trail is quaint and covered and provides lots of shade in the summer months.

Weedon Island Preserve Trail
Difficulty 1

Hike this 4.3-mile loop trail in Weedon Island Preserve near St. Petersburg. The hike is mostly paved or elevated with a boardwalk and provides several lookouts along the way.

The Circle B Bar Reserve has a very active bird population in the winter months.

Circle B Bar Reserve Trail
Difficulty 2

Hike or walk this 4.8-mile loop trail in Circle B Bar Reserve near Highland City in central Florida.

Not much separates you from the wildlife of the region along the Shark Valley Tram Trail.

Shark Valley Tram Trail
Difficulty 2

Hike, run, bike, and bird watch along this 15.8-mile loop trail through Everglades National Park. This paved trail cuts through the center of the Everglades freshwater marsh and is subject to flooding when the water levels are high.

The clear water at Wekiwa Springs is a sign of just how valuable the natural resource is to the state of Florida.

Wekiwa Springs Orange Trail
Difficulty 3

Hike this 6.3-mile loop trail in Wekiwa Springs State Park near Apopka to see a variety of wildlife including turtles, snakes, deer, and turkeys. Take a dip in Wekiwa Springs to cool down.

A view of the boardwalk meandering through Robinson's Preserve.

Robinson's Preserve Trail
Difficulty 3

Hike this 7.5-mile loop trail in Robinson's Preserve near Cortez to follow this single-track boardwalk through the mangroves.

Georgia

Georgia is the twenty-fourth largest state in the United States and is located in the South along the Atlantic Coast. It has nearly 100 miles of coastline as well as fourteen barrier islands. From the coastline, the state of Georgia ascends from its low-lying coastal plain, which covers nearly the entirety of the southern half of the state, into the Piedmont Plateau and the foothills of the Blue Ridge Mountains. As you continue to move west the Appalachian Mountains distinguish themselves from the Blue Ridge Mountains. These two mountain ranges cover the northern section of Georgia and offer a number of ecologies to explore. The tallest point in the state is Brasstown Bald at 4,784 feet above sea level and is located in the Blue Ridge Mountains.

Hiking in Georgia is always better in the fall to escape the heat and experience the leaves changing color.

Mount Yonah Trail
Difficulty 4

Hike this 4.2-mile out-and-back trail in Chattahoochee-Oconee National Forest near Cleveland to ascend nearly 1,400 feet to the summit of Mt. Yonah. You will experience a difficult yet fulfilling hike into the mountains of northern Georgia.

The Raven Cliff Wilderness is located in Chattahoochee National Forest and contains nearly 41 miles of streams that are perfect for trout fishing.

Raven Cliff Falls Trail
Difficulty 3

Hike this 5.8-mile out-and-back trail in the Raven Cliffs Wilderness near Helen. The trail remains relatively flat along Dodd Creek. Steep ascents begin at the end of the trail to reach where Matthews Creek falls over Raven Cliff.

Blood Mountain & Freeman Loop Trail
Difficulty 4

Hike this 5.7-mile loop trail in the Blood Mountain Wilderness near Blairsville to ascend nearly 1,500 feet to the summit of Blood Mountain. You can hike this trail year round, but it is recommended to hike in the summer due to the several streams you have to cross along the way.

The deep forests of Blood Mountain Wilderness are a part of the Chattahoochee National Forest.

There is a beautiful observatory at the top of Brasstown Bald for you to relax and take in the views.

Brasstown Bald Trail
Difficulty 3

Hike this 7-mile out-and-back trail to the summit of Georgia's highest point, Brasstown Bald. From the lower parking lot you will ascend up this paved trail along its 12% inclines and switchbacks. From the top, you can see the expanse of rolling hills of northern Georgia.

The falls along Big Creek are created by a spillway dam, not a natural rock formation.

Vickery Creek Trail
Difficulty 2

Hike this 3.4-mile loop trail in the Vickery Creek Unit of Chattahoochee River National Recreation Area near Roswell. Big Creek is a great swimming hole for hikers, but it is not recommended to swim near the falls.

The Amicalola Falls descend nearly 430 feet and are one of the tallest falls in the state.

East Ridge Loop Trail
Difficulty 2

Hike this 2-mile loop trail in Amicalola Falls State Park near Marble Hill. You'll ascend only 784 feet to reach the top of Amicalola Falls.

Dukes Creek is the place where gold was first found in White County, Georgia, which led to the 1828 Georgia Gold Rush.

Dukes Creek Trail
Difficulty 2

Hike this 2.3-mile out-and-back trail in Chattahoochee-Oconee National Forest near Helen to the bottom of the ravine where Dukes Creek flows. The trail features a waterfall, like many trails in Georgia, and there are benches near the falls to relax and take in the views.

A nice swimming pool under a cascading waterfall in Daniel's Creek in Cloudland Canyon State Park.

Sitton's Gulch Trail
Difficulty 4

Hike this 5-mile out-and-back trail in the Cloudland Canyon State Park near Trenton and ascend nearly 1,000 feet as you hike in and back out of Sitton's Gulch. Swimming is a popular way to rest along the trail.

The Chattahoochee River runs for nearly 430 miles and empties into the Apalachicola Bay off the Gulf Shore of Florida's panhandle.

East Palisades Trail
Difficulty 3

Hike this 3.3-mile loop trail located in Chattahoochee River National Recreation Area near Atlanta to see beautiful views of the Chattahoochee River. You can walk, run, or hike along high bluffs to look down upon the majestic river.

Here we see a suspended bridge at Tallulah Gorge State Park spanning over the gorge.

North and South Rim Loop Trail
Difficulty 2

Hike this 1.8-mile loop trail through Tallulah Gorge State Park near Tallulah Falls. Along the way you'll see several waterfalls, including Tallulah Falls, and the deep forests of northern Georgia.

Hawaii

Hawaii is the forty-seventh largest state in the United States and is the only state that is entirely made of islands. It is also the only state solely located in the tropics. There are eight main islands in the Hawaii archipelago, and only six are inhabited. Aside from the eight main islands, there are numerous smaller islands that also compose the archipelago. There are several active volcanoes in the state, and the islands themselves were made from volcanic magma deposits of the Hawaiian Volcanic Hotspot. The highest point in the state is Mauna Kea, which rises nearly 13,800 feet above sea level.

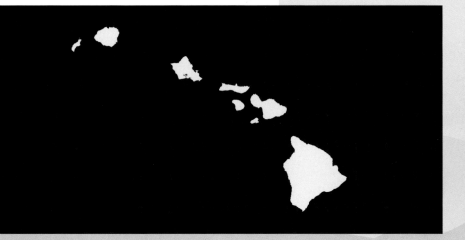

The Diamond Head Summit Trail was built in 1908 and is paved all the way to the rim of the crater.

Diamond Head Summit Trail
Difficulty 2
Hike this 1.8-mile out-and-back trail at Diamond Head State Monument near Honolulu on the island of Oahu. Hike just a few hundred feet up to the Diamond Head Crater that has a diameter of 3,500 feet and is an indication of Hawaii's still active volcanic history.

Be careful if you decide to go swimming at Makapu'u Beach, because it has been rated as one of Oahu's most dangerous beaches.

Makapu'u Point Lighthouse Trail
Difficulty 2
Hike this 2.5-mile out-and-back trail near Waimea on the island of Oahu to hike to the remote lighthouse that shines out over the Pacific Ocean. Along this paved trail, you have grand views of the coast before you reach the historic lighthouse.

Manoa Falls descends nearly 150 feet to the pool below. Swimming in the pool is discouraged due to the likelihood of contracting Leptospirosis, which causes flu-like symptoms.

Manoa Falls Trail
Difficulty 2
Hike this 1.7-mile out-and-back trail in Round Top Forest Reserve near Honolulu on the island of Oahu. You'll ascend quickly to the base of the falls through thick rainforest that seems like it's from a movie.

The Waimoku Waterfall is 400 feet high.

Pipiwai Trail
Difficulty 3
Hike this 3.8-mile out-and-back trail in Haleakala National Park near Hana on the island of Maui to pass several waterfalls before you reach the grand Waimoku Falls at the end of the trail. You'll walk the boardwalk through thick bamboo forests.

Climbing to the top of Mount Olomana is only recommended for experienced hikers.

Olomana Trail
Difficulty 5

Hike this 4.4-mile out-and-back trail in Mount Olomana State Monument near Kailua on the island of Oahu. Ascend nearly 1,800 feet to summit three peaks, including Mount Olomana.

Visit Lanikai Beach on weekdays for a less crowded experience, and take care to avoid parking illegally in nearby residential areas.

Lanikai Pillbox Trail
Difficulty 3

Also called the Kaiwa Ridge Trail, this out-and-back hike is short at 1.7 miles but offers a moderate challenge and great views of Oahu, Kailua Beach, and Lanikai Beach. It's a popular hike, so expect to encounter others as you go.

A view of one of the swimming holes in the Oheo Gulch.

Seven Sacred Pools Trail
Difficulty 1

Hike this .6-mile loop trail in Haleakala National Park near Hana on the island of Maui to hike along seven swimming pools in the Oheo Gulch with ocean views in the distance. Make sure to check the conditions before you go with expectations to swim because the pools can close due to flash flooding.

An aerial view of the black sand beach at the Wai'anapanapa State Park.

Sea Caves & Black Sand Beach Trail
Difficulty 1

Hike this .6-mile out-and-back trail in Wai'anapanapa State Park near Hana on the island of Maui to visit the secluded black sand beach of the park.

The West Maui Forest Reserve is incredibly beautiful in its diversity.

Waihe'e Ridge Trail
Difficulty 5

Hike this 4-mile out-and-back trail in West Maui Forest Reserve near Wailuku on the island of Maui. Ascend nearly 1,600 feet to reach the ridgeline for great views of the ocean and breathtaking trail passes.

Kuliouou Ridge Trail
Difficulty 4

Hike this 4.7-mile out-and-back trail in Kuliouou Forest Reserve near Honolulu on the island of Oahu to climb up to and along the steep Kuliouou Ridge. You'll ascend nearly 1,800 feet to reach the ridge, but be prepared when you get to the top because the rocks can be slippery when wet, and the dropoffs are steep.

Idaho

Idaho is the fourteenth largest state in the United States and ranks thirty-eighth in terms of population size. Its northern panhandle has historically been a very isolated region in the United States and is even hard to access from the more populated Snake River Plateau in southern Idaho. The Rocky Mountains form many of the rugged landscapes found in Idaho, and many of the east-to-west ranges of the Rockies physically separate the north and south sections of the state. Idaho is home to the largest area of federally protected wilderness, the Frank Church-River of No Return Wilderness Area, which connects 2.3 million acres of contiguous land in central Idaho. There are several national forests in the state, including the Payette, Challis, Salmon, and Bitterroot National Forests.

Alice Lake is nearly 8,600 feet above sea level and can remain frozen well into June some years.

Tin Cup Hiker

Difficulty 5

Hike this 20-mile loop in Sawtooth National Recreation Area near Stanley to backpack or camp in the Idaho wilderness. Hike past several alpine lakes including Alice, Toxaway, and Farley Lakes with epic "sawtooth" rock formations towering above.

Be sure to bring winter gear while visiting the Sawtooth Mountains after October or before June.

Iron Creek Stanley Lake Trail
Difficulty 4

Hike this 10-mile out-and-back trail in Sawtooth National Forest near Stanley to climb nearly 1,800 feet into the Sawtooth Mountains. Make your way to the banks of Sawtooth Lake and take in the views.

A view of Lake Coeur d'Alene from the Mineral Ridge Trail.

Mineral Ridge National Recreation Trail
Difficulty 2

Hike this 3-mile loop trail near Coeur d'Alene to climb above Wolf Lodge Bay of Lake Coeur d'Alene. There are plenty of places at the end of the trail to sit and relax to take in the beauty.

The Idaho Panhandle National Forest is home to several species of wildlife, including black and grizzly bears, white-tailed deer, coyotes, moose, timber wolves, bobcats, cougars, wolverines, beavers, elk, and more. Use caution while hiking.

Marie Creek Trail
Difficulty 4

Hike this 8.7-mile out-and-back trail through Idaho Panhandle National Forest near Coeur d'Alene and walk along Marie Creek. You'll ascend nearly 1,500 feet past pastures of wildflowers and deep into the woods.

There are several pools along the Goldbug Hot Springs Trail. Some springs are hot, some are cold, and some are a mix of both hot and cold water.

Goldbug Hot Springs Trail
Difficulty 2

Hike 3.5-mile out-and-back trail in Salmon National Forest near Salmon, Idaho, to take a dip in natural hot springs. You only have to climb about 1,000 feet up the sagebrush-lined hills to get to this secluded outdoor sauna.

Idaho Panhandle National Forest, at an elevation above 8,000 feet, is prone to cold and erratic weather most of the year.

Stevens Lakes Trail
Difficulty 4

Hike this 5-mile trail in Idaho Panhandle National Forest near Mullan and climb nearly 1,800 feet into the rocky wilderness to two secluded alpine lakes. This area is great for fly-fishing and camping.

Gold was discovered in Boise National Forest in the 1860s, and mining continued until the mid-twentieth century.

Adelmann Mine & Lucky Peak Trail
Difficulty 4

Hike this 8.8-mile out-and-back trail in Boise National Forest and ascend nearly 2,400 feet past an old gold mine to the summit of Shaw Mountain. You'll cross grasslands and steppes of sagebrush as you explore the rolling mountainsides outside of Boise.

You will see stunning spires towering above you along the Ship Island Lake Trail in Salmon Naitonal Forest.

Ship Island Lake Trail
Difficulty 5
Hike this 20.4-mile out-and-back trail in Salmon National Forest near Cobalt to adventure into Idaho's Bighorn Crags region of the Salmon River Mountains. This trail is perfect for a multi-day backpacking trip as you adventure in the rugged and rocky mountain sides toward Ship Island Lake. Be careful though, you'll ascend nearly 6,300 feet before you get to the lake.

The Box Canyon Springs cut through the high plains of southern Idaho and offer a beautiful place to swim.

Box Canyon Springs Trail
Difficulty 2
Hike this 4.3-mile loop trail in Box Canyon Springs Preserve near Wendell to visit the springs that come flowing out of the area's underground aquifer and into the Snake River. Go dipping in the ice cold water at the end of the trail.

Redfish Lake along the Bench Lakes Trail during a foggy winter morning.

Bench Lakes Trail
Difficulty 4
Hike this 7.8-mile trail and ascend nearly 1,200 feet in Sawtooth National Forest near Stanley. You'll start along Redfish Lake with the mountains on one side and the lake on the other before you climb a little higher to reach the smaller lakes above. Beautiful views await.

Illinois

Illinois is the twenty-fifth largest state in the United States and ranks sixth in terms of population size. Northern Illinois is dominated by Chicago and its suburbs radiating from the state's short shoreline along Lake Michigan. In far northwestern Illinois you will find the southern extent of the Driftless Area, a region in Iowa, Wisconsin, and Minnesota that is extremely hilly because it was untouched by the last ice age. Illinois' western border consists almost entirely of the Mississippi River.

Although it doesn't really compare to the Grand Canyon, the Little Grand Canyon is nice for Illinois.

Little Grand Canyon
Difficulty 3
Hike this 3.4-mile loop trail in Shawnee National Forest near Ponoma in southern Illinois to see an unexpected canyon carved through the region's sandy soil. This little box canyon rests on the banks of the Big Muddy River and can be quite slippery after it rains.

Jackson Falls Trail
Difficulty 3
Hike this 4.2-mile loop trail in Shawnee National Forest near Simpson to wander through the hardwood forest and to the beautiful Jackson Falls along Little Bay Creek.

Giant City Nature Trail
Difficulty 1
Hike this 1-mile loop trail through Giant City State Park near Makanda to walk below giant bluffs along a quiet stream.

Along the Rim Rock Trail, you can choose to stay on the top of the rim and walk the canyon from the top, or descend into the canyon and explore the caves and crevices.

Rim Rock Recreation Trail
Difficulty 3
Hike this 1.7-mile trail in Shawnee National Forest near Junction to walk along the edge of one of the area's many canyons. You'll climb under bluffs and around rock formations in this quiet section of the forest.

The Shawnee National Forest consists of second-growth forest from the 1930s after agriculture left the area.

Garden of the Gods Loop
Difficulty 2

Hike this 6.3-mile loop trail around Garden of the Gods Recreation Area in Shawnee National Forest near Equality to see the stunning rock formations of southern Illinois. Explore in between the gray sandstone hoodoos and rock formations along the way.

Waterfalls tumble into Dells Canyon after summer rains, and icefalls form in the winter.

Dells Canyon & Bluff Trail
Difficulty 2

Hike this 2-mile out-and-back trail through Matthiessen State Park near Oglesby to explore the deep sandstone canyons of central Illinois. Dug by the estuaries of the Illinois River, this area is filled with box canyons to be explored.

The waterfalls in Starved Rock State Park aren't always falling, but be sure to visit after it has rained to see them in action.

French Canyon Trail
Difficulty 3

Hike this 2.5-mile out-and-back trail in Starved Rock State Park near Utica to explore this beautiful canyon nestled along the banks of the Illinois River.

A photo of Ferne Clyffe Waterfall after a storm.

Ferne Clyffe Waterfall Trail
Difficulty 2

Hike this 1.3-mile trail in Ferne Clyffe State Park near Goreville in southern Illinois to explore the bluffsides and waterfalls of Shawnee National Forest.

The Swallow Cliff Woods offers lush greenery just outside of the city.

Sag Valley Yellow Loop Trail
Difficulty 3

Hike this 7.6-mile loop trail in Swallow Cliff Woods near Palos Parks in the suburbs of Chicago to see a bluff left by the last glaciation nearly 12,000 years ago.

The beautiful water along Waterfall Glen Trail in the suburbs of Chicago.

Waterfall Glen Trail
Difficulty 3

Hike, run, walk, or bike this 9-mile trail in the western Chicago suburb of Darien to get away from the city for the day. Visit the small, tumbling waterfall along Sawmill Creek.

Indiana

Indiana is the thirty-eighth largest state in the United States. The state's northern region features rolling hills and flat prairies that were formed by the last glaciation. Around the shores of Lake Michigan, sand dunes offer beachgoers majestic formations that are more difficult to climb than you would imagine. This area has some of the state's highest elevations, ranging from 600–1,000 feet above sea level. As we move south into central Indiana, the elevations get lower, and the hills of the north recede into long, shallow agricultural valleys. Southern Indiana is more forested than northern Indiana, and the hills in this region are steeper than the other two regions. Both the Wabash and Ohio Rivers form long, flat valleys in the region. The state is home to several state and national forests, and even a newly established national park at the Indiana Dunes along the shores of Lake Michigan.

Lake Michigan's eastern coast is home to the largest freshwater sand dune system in the world.

Cowles Bog Trail
Difficulty 3
Hike this 4.3-mile loop trail in Indiana Dunes National Park near Portage to experience the region's towering sand dunes along the shores of Lake Michigan. You'll pass through black oak savannas, bogs, swamps, and pastures of wildflowers.

Lake Monroe is the state's largest lake that is entirely within the state's borders.

Lake Monroe Peninsula Trail
Difficulty 3
Hike this 10.1-mile out-and-back trail in Charles C. Deam Wilderness near Norman. You can hike this trail and backpack for a few days, or you can mountain bike the trail in one day. The trail is mostly downhill on the way in toward the lake, so be prepared for the uphill walk on the way out.

Tiny pocket caves found in the walls of the Hemlock Cliffs in Hoosier National Forest.

Hemlock Cliffs National Scenic Trail
Difficulty 2
Hike this 1.2-mile loop trail in Hoosier National Forest near English. Hike down into the slot canyons and enjoy the quiet forests of hemlock and oak.

Wolves inhabited Indiana in the 1800s, and the cave garnered its name from the wolves that used to live inside it.

While you're exploring Clifty Falls State Park, be sure to check out the abandoned and never-finished railroad tunnel.

Tunnel Falls Loop Trail
Difficulty 4

Hike this 5.4-mile loop trail in Clifty Falls State Park and ascend nearly 1,050 feet. Along the way you'll walk by several waterfalls, including Tunnel, Hoffman, and Clifty Falls.

Wolf Cave Trail
Difficulty 3

Hike this 2-mile loop trail in McCormick's Creek State Park near Spencer to find the beautiful Wolf Cave. Check first, as tornado damage caused closures in 2023.

You'll cross streams and climb down ladders to maneuver the terrain of Turkey Run State Park.

Turkey Run Outer Loop
Difficulty 3

Hike this 6-mile loop trail in Turkey Run State Park near Marshall. You'll see the state's best terrain as you make your way through deep ravines and over ridge tops.

The Dune Succession Trail is short, but it can be difficult for those not prepared for all of the stairs.

Dune Succession Trail
Difficulty 2

Hike this 1.2-mile trail through the dunes of Indiana Dunes National Park near Portage and learn about the four stages of dune development along the way. Climb nearly 250 stairs to gain excellent views of Lake Michigan and then hang out for the day at West Beach.

Three Lakes Trail
Difficulty 4

Hike this 10-mile loop trail in Morgan Monroe State Forest near Martinsville and ascend nearly 1,082 feet toward the shores of three lakes nestled in the forest. The trail can be muddy after if it's rained, or the creek can dry up if it hasn't.

Pate Hollow Trail
Difficulty 3

Hike this 6.1-mile loop trail in Hoosier National Forest near Smithville and enjoy the beautiful forest.

Lawrence Creek Trail
Difficulty 2

Hike this 4.5-mile trail in Fort Harrison State Park near Indianapolis and explore the woodlands and deep ravines of the area. Be sure to bring solid footwear because the path can be very muddy.

Iowa

Iowa is the twenty-sixth largest state in the United States and is located nearly smack dab in the middle of the contiguous United States. Much of its land features gentle rolling hills and flat prairie grasslands that are mostly used for agriculture today. Iowa is home to a large meteor impact that hit Earth nearly seventy-four million years ago. Although the last ice age and glaciation removed any evidence of the impact crater, the Decorah Crater is believed to have been 3.5 miles in diameter, and the impact would have killed anything within 650 miles of the impact site. The state features several landforms, including the Paleozoic Plateau, the Des Moines Lobe, the Southern Drift Plain, the Mississippian Alluvial Plain, and the Loess Hills. There are several paleontological sites in the state due to the ancient bedrock in the state, with some areas dating to 500 million years into the past.

A view from the Hitchcock Nature Center Loop Trail with the observation tower seen in the distance.

Maquoketa Caves State Park has more caves than any other state park in the United States.

Here we see the Hidden Cave along the Wildcat Den Trail in Wildcat Den State Park.

Cedar trees and bluffs surrounding the Cedar River make the Palisades-Kepler State Park something to behold.

Hitchcock Nature Center Loop Trail
Difficulty 4
Hike this 6.4-mile loop trail in Hitchcock Nature Area near Honey Creek and ascend nearly 1,200 feet. You'll climb up and over the rolling hills of the Loess Hills region.

Maquoketa Caves Loop
Difficulty 2
Hike this 1.7-mile loop trail in Maquoketa Caves State Park near Maquoketa. You can explore the caves in the state park and crawl through the mud and water to find new passageways underground.

Wildcat Den Trail
Difficulty 3
Hike this 4-mile trail in Wildcat Den State Park near Muscatine to see a variety of terrain and a number of rock formations like Steamboat Rock, Devil's Punch Bowl, and Fat Man Squeeze.

Cedar Cliff Trail
Difficulty 2
Hike this 2.1-mile out-and-back trail in Palisades-Kepler State Park near Mount Vernon. You'll journey along the banks of the Cedar River and under the dense canopy of trees that line the way.

A photo of the High Trestle Bridge crossing the Des Moines River along the High Trestle Trail.

Brown's Woods Trail
Difficulty 2

Hike, run, or walk this 3.2-mile trail in Brown's Woods near West Des Moines, located just outside the city limits. You'll walk the banks of the Raccoon River and across several streams through the lovely preserve.

High Trestle Trail
Difficulty 3

Hike, walk, run, or bike this 24-mile trail that connects the cities of Ankeny and Woodward. You'll cross the Des Moines River and pass through pristine Iowan countryside.

Mines of Spain State Park offers wetlands, forests, creeks, and cropland to explore and provides some of the best wildlife watching in the state.

Here we see the Maquoketa River flowing below the West Lake and East Lake Trail Loop. Backbone State Park offers nearly 21-miles of trails for hiking.

Raccoon River Park offers beaches for swimming, a boat launch, hiking trails, shoreline fishing, and many other activities.

Sandstone shelves rise out of the ground, sometimes at more than 100 feet, all through Ledges State Park.

Horseshoe Bluff Nature Trail
Difficulty 1

Hike this .9-mile loop trail in Mines of Spain State Park near Dubuque to see grand views of the Mississippi River from the bluffs above its waters.

West Lake & East Lake Trail Loop
Difficulty 3

Hike this 6.3-mile loop trail in Backbone State Park near Dundee. You'll walk along the Maquoketa River and then to the shores of Backbone Lake through the Backbone State Park wilderness.

Blue Heron Lake Loop Trail
Difficulty 2

Hike this 3.3-mile loop trail in Raccoon River Park near West Des Moines to walk around the entirety of Blue Heron Lake.

Canyon Road and Table Rock Loop
Difficulty 2

Hike this 1.7-mile loop trail through Ledges State Park near Boone to see beautiful outcroppings of sandstone and dense forests.

Kansas

Kansas is the fifteenth largest state in the United States and is known for its large swaths of Midwestern Plains. Nearly two-thirds of the state is a part of the Great Central Plain of the United States, or the Great Plains, while the eastern third of the state is dominated by rolling hills. The state's elevation gently rises from east to west as you approach the Colorado border in the west. The eastern half of the state lies at about 700 feet and the western portion of the state reaches nearly 4,000 feet above sea level at Mount Sunflower. Kansas is home to several important waterways including the Missouri, Kansas, and Arkansas Rivers and has several of its natural areas conserved and managed by the state or federal government.

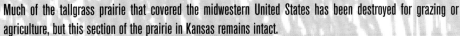
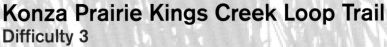
Much of the tallgrass prairie that covered the midwestern United States has been destroyed for grazing or agriculture, but this section of the prairie in Kansas remains intact.

White-tail deer grazing in Wyandotte County Lake Park.

Konza Prairie Kings Creek Loop Trail
Difficulty 3
Hike this 4.6-mile trail in Konza Prairie Natural Area near Manhattan along the timber-lined Kings Creek and then emerge into the Flint Hills Tallgrass Prairie. You might see buffalo roaming the prairie along with curious prairie dogs peeping out of their burrows.

Wyandotte County Lake Lookout Trail
Difficulty 4
Hike this 9.7-mile loop trail in Wyandotte County Lake Park near Kansas City to journey around the shores of Wyandotte Lake. You'll ascend nearly 1,200 feet, so prepare for some incline in this supposedly flat state.

The Kansas River runs quietly through the center of Lawrence. The Kansas River Trail follows the river outside of the city to the east.

Kansas River Trail
Difficulty 2
Hike, run, bike, or walk this 8-mile gravel trail outside of Lawrence along the banks of the Kansas River.

Water flowing quickly down Indian Creek after spring storms.

Indian Creek Trail
Difficulty 3
Hike, run, walk, or bike this 22.5-mile paved trail through Kansas City and Overland Park along Indian Creek in eastern Kansas. There are several different landscapes you'll pass along the way, and there is plenty of shade for hot days.

Kanopolis Lake State Park features sandstone canyons, prairies, the Kanopolis Reservoir, and the Smoky Hill River. All provide a scenic backdrop for exploring the frontier.

Horse Thief Trail
Difficulty 2
Hike this 1.9-mile loop trail in Kanopolis Lake State Park near Kanopolis in the Smoky Hills region of eastern Kansas. This area has unique sandstone canyons that spur from the banks of the Smoky Hill River and Kanopolis Reservoir.

The Tomahawk Creek Trail is very popular for runners and bikers and is used year round.

Tomahawk Creek Trail
Difficulty 3
Hike, run, bike, or walk this 12.8-mile paved trail outside of Leawood in the southern suburbs of Kansas City.

The Gary L. Haller National Recreation Trail crosses paths with several road and highways, but crosses them by an underpass or overpass so pedestrians don't have to deal with traffic.

Gary L. Haller National Recreation Trail
Difficulty 3
Hike, walk, bike, or run this 13-mile trail in Mill Creek Streamway Park near Edwardsville. This paved trail provides great opportunities to see the countryside in eastern Kansas.

Lake Lenexa Trail
Difficulty 1
Hike or walk this 2.1-mile loop trail in Black Hoof Park in Lenexa around the shores of Lake Lenexa.

Turkey Creek Trail
Difficulty 3
Hike, run, or bike this 7.2-mile out-and-back trail near Overland Park in eastern Kansas to follow Turkey Creek. You'll pass gardens, prairies, parks, and a waterfall.

Elk River Hiking Trail
Difficulty 4
Hike this 15-mile out-and-back trail along Elk River in Elk City State Park and ascend nearly 1,000 feet along the way. You'll cross several streams and enjoy views along the banks of Elk City Lake.

Kentucky

Kentucky is the thirty-seventh largest state in the United States. It's famous for its pastures of bluegrass, its horses, and its bourbon. There are five main regions in the state, including the mountainous Cumberland Plateau in the east, the Outer Bluegrass, the Mississippi Plateau, the Jackson Purchase, and the Western Coal Fields. The Cumberland Plateau features the rugged Appalachian Mountains, filled with deep verdant valleys and several of the state's historical coal mines. The Outer Bluegrass region is an extremely fertile area that consists of rolling hills and Kentucky pastures famous for raising horses. The Mississippi Plateau features a karst topography that creates the area's numerous caves and rocky outcroppings. The Western Coal Fields provide many of the state's modern coal mines, while the Jackson Purchase region composes the state's western border along the Mississippi River. The state houses one national park, several dozen state parks, two national forests, and several national historic sites and recreation areas. Kentucky is home to several major rivers, including the Mississippi, Tennessee, Big Sandy, Cumberland, Ohio, and Kentucky Rivers. There are plenty of outdoor recreation opportunities in the state including white water rafting, hiking, mountain biking, backpacking, and fishing.

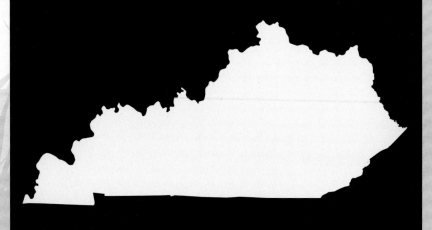

Be sure to visit in the spring after it rains to see Van Hook Falls in all of its glory.

Van Hook Falls & Cane Creek Valley Trail
Difficulty 3

Hike this 5.7-mile out-and-back trail in Daniel Boone National Forest near London to hike along Cane Creek to the majestic Van Hook Falls. You'll climb into Cane Creek Valley around its large slabs of stone where you can sit for a rest and listen to the water tumble by.

You'll not only see the Double Arch along the Auxier Ridge Trail, but you'll also see several other beautiful Red River Gorge rock formations like Courthouse Rock.

Auxier Ridge Loop
Difficulty 4

Hike this 6-mile loop in Daniel Boone National Forest in eastern Kentucky near Stanton and ascend nearly 1,000 feet into the Appalachian Mountains. You'll climb up through a forest of hemlocks and bigleaf magnolias to the Double Arch and then double back to see Courthouse Rock.

Because of the area's sandstone deposits, the Red River Gorge and Daniel Boone National Forest are hotspots for rock climbers to visit. There are more than 100 arches found in this region.

Gray's Arch Trail Loop
Difficulty 2

Hike this 3.4-mile loop trail in Daniel Boone National Forest near Slade to see another of the national forest's many natural stone archways. It is suggested to follow the loop counterclockwise in order to see the best views of the gorge on your way down to the arch.

Dog Slaughter Falls turns gently over the ridge and falls fifteen feet into the pool below.

Dog Slaughter Falls Trail
Difficulty 2

Hike this 2.4-mile out-and-back trail in Cumberland Falls State Park near Corbin to follow along Dog Slaughter Creek toward the falls. You meander through thickets of rhododendrons and hemlocks and over some pretty large boulders to get to the falls.

Rock Bridge is the only natural arch in the Red River Gorge that crosses a body of water.

Rock Bridge Trail
Difficulty 2

Hike this 1.4-mile loop trail in Clifty Wilderness near Pine Ridge to follow along one of the area's most beautiful trails. Along the way, you'll pass Creation Falls along Swift Camp Creek. After that you'll make your way to the Rock Bridge.

The sandstone bedrock of this area provides the perfect medium for natural archways to be carved by millions of years of erosion.

Sky Bridge Red River Gorge
Difficulty 2

Hike this 8-mile loop trail in Daniel Boone National Forest near Pine Ridge to see one of the area's grandest arches. If you're feeling adventurous, climb on top of the arch once you've explored it from below.

Backpackers scrambling down the Indian Staircase Trail.

Indian Staircase Trail
Difficulty 3

Hike this 3.1-mile trail in Daniel Boone National Forest near Frenchburg to climb the steep Indian Staircase. You'll scramble up along the sandstone outcropping to the bald top of the ridge. At the top, go see the Cloudsplitter rock formation.

There are plenty of campsites along the Copperas Falls Trail if you want to stay the night and hang out along the banks of the waterfall's pool.

Copperas Falls Trail
Difficulty 2

Hike this 3.1-mile out-and-back trail in Clifty Wilderness near Pine Ridge to see another magnificent waterfall. You'll have to cross the creek several times along the way, and the trail can often be muddy, so bring your hiking boots.

A photo of the Smoky Bridge along the Three Bridge Trail in Carter Caves State Resort Park.

Three Bridges Trail
Difficulty 3

Hike this 3.1-mile loop trail in Carter Caves State Resort Park near Olive Hill in northeastern Kentucky. Enjoy all of the beautiful rock formations along the way including Fern Bridge, Smoky Bridge, and Raven Bridge.

Cumberland Falls crashes nearly sixty-nine feet to the river below. The falls are also called "Little Niagara," or "Great Falls."

Eagle Falls Trail
Difficulty 2
Hike this 1.8-mile loop trail in Cumberland Falls State Park near Parkers Lake to not only see Eagle Falls depositing into the Cumberland River, but also the thundering Cumberland Falls.

Louisiana

Louisiana is the thirty-first largest state in the United States. The southern end of the state is a low-lying alluvial coastal plain filled with swamps and wetlands. The Mississippi River Delta creates much of this alluvial plain, and the state has lost nearly 1,800 square miles of land along the Gulf Coast due to erosion and rising sea levels. This section of the state is the fastest-disappearing area in the world due to coastal and resource mismanagement. The northern Uplands of the state support lush forests and prairies. The highest point in the state is Driskill Mountain, standing at nearly 535 feet above sea level.

Cedars standing along Gorge Run Trail in Bogue Chitto State Park.

The Backbone Trail is rocky and sandy and surrounded by longleaf pines. Piney hills are surrounded by hardwood bottoms in this region of the Louisiana Uplands.

Gorge Run Trail
Difficulty 3
Hike this 5.7-mile loop trail in Bogue Chitto State Park near Franklinton in southeastern Louisiana. You can explore the upper and lower parts of the gorge, but be sure to watch for mountain bikers zipping along the path.

Backbone Trail
Difficulty 3
Hike this 10.6-mile loop trail in Kisatchie National Forest near Mora to make it to the Longleaf Vista Road and take in the spectacular views of rolling hills and rocky outcroppings.

Wild Azalea Trail
Difficulty 5
Hike this 23.9-mile trail in Kisatchie National Forest between Woodworth and Valentine Lake and ascend nearly 1,700 feet along the way. You can camp at Evangeline Camp and then make your way to the shores of Valentine Lake on day two.

Tammany Trace Trail
Difficulty 2
Hike or bike this 27.1-mile paved rail-trail in Fontainebleau State Park near Covington. This trail is good for people of all experience levels and provides sweeping views of the northside of Lake Pontchartrain.

A photo of the Comite River in Comite River Park.

Comite Park Trail
Difficulty 3

Hike this 5.1-mile loop trail in Comite River Park near Baton Rouge in southern Louisiana. This park is very popular for mountain biking but it also provides several great trails for hiking and leisurely walks.

The Cane Bayou is home to horned owls, ospreys, and several other bird species. And of course, beware of alligators in the waters below.

Cane Bayou Track
Difficulty 2

Hike this 3.7-mile trail in Fontainebleau State Park near Mandeville in southeastern Louisiana. The bayou is located across Lake Pontchartrain from New Orleans and offers several spots for fishing and wildlife watching.

A tiny waterfall in Tunica Hills State Wildlife Management Area.

Tunica Hills C Trail
Difficulty 2

Hike this 3.6-mile trail through Tunica Hills State Wildlife Management Area near Francisville. You'll follow the stream for about a mile before you dive into the surrounding forest. The area is very popular for hunting and requires a permit to enter.

Cypress trees growing off the shores and in the middle of Lake Chicot.

Lake Chicot Loop Trail
Difficulty 4

Hike this 17.4-mile loop trail in the Chicot State Park near Ville Platte in central Louisiana. The cool waters of Lake Chicot are home to record-breaking largemouth bass, bluegill, and sunfish, so bring your fishing pole.

Beware of gators in the waters below the boardwalk in Jean Lafitte National Historical Park and Preserve.

Bayou Coquille & Marsh Overlook Trail
Difficulty 1

Hike this 1.9-mile out-and-back trail in Jean Lafitte National Historical Park and Preserve near Marrero in southern Louisiana. Walk along the boardwalk trail on the banks of the Bayou Coquille to then look over the grand marsh that stretches before your eyes.

A female anhinga sitting on a branch looking over Big Branch Marsh.

Boy Scout Road Trail
Difficulty 3

Hike this 5-mile trail in Big Branch Marsh National Wildlife Refuge near Lacombe on the northern shores of Lake Pontchartrain. You'll meander through forests and then along the swamps and marshes of the area. The trail is used for both hiking and mountain biking, so beware of cyclists zipping by.

Maine

Maine is the thirty-ninth largest state in the United States, and is the country's easternmost state located between the Canadian border to the north and the Atlantic Ocean to the southeast. It only borders one other state, Vermont, and is the only state in the nation to do so. Much of the state's Atlantic Ocean coastline is rugged and rocky and features several cliffsides, bays, inlets, and lighthouses. The interior of the state is filled with gently rolling mountain ranges, dense and expansive forests, and elegant waterways. Maine remains the most forested state in the United States and is also the least populated state east of the Mississippi River. Much of the state's topography was greatly influenced by the end of the last ice age, which created many of the geologic formations found in Acadia National Park, including Somes Sound, Bubble Rock, and Mount Desert Island. Maine's interior suffers from extremely cold and snowy winters and humid summers, while the coast of Maine is more temperate with milder winters and cooler summers. There are plenty of outdoor recreation activities to participate in, summer or winter, snow or shine.

There are several sections of rung ladders on your way up the Beehive. Once at the top, you can see Bar Harbor and the Atlantic Ocean behind you and Bowl Pond in front of you.

On the Mount Katahdin & Hamlin Peak Loop, you'll walk between summits on Maine's highest mountain in Baxter State Park.

The Beehive Loop trail
Difficulty 3
Hike this 1.5-mile loop trail in Acadia National Park near Bar Harbor where you use rung ladders to climb over the Beehive rock formation and then to the shores of Bowl Pond. It is recommended you go around the loop counterclockwise to go up the rung ladders, considering it is much more difficult to work your way down them.

Mount Katahdin & Hamlin Peak Loop
Difficulty 5
Hike this 10.9-mile loop trail in Baxter State Park near Millinocket where you will ascend nearly 4,475 feet and summit Maine's highest mountain, Baxter Mountain. Along the trail you will summit three peaks in total and make a stop at Chimney Pond nestled in prime alpine New England.

Baxter State Park offers visitors a pristine forest filled with tumbling streams and waterfalls.

Appalachian Trail to Little Big Niagara Falls
Difficulty 2
Hike this 2.3-mile stretch of the Appalachian Trail in Baxter State Park near Millinocket to see the Little and Big Niagara Falls. You'll start from the Daicey Pond Campground and meander through the forest toward two sets of falls along Nes Owandehunk Stream.

A view from the summit of Puzzle Mountain.

Puzzle Mountain Trail
Difficulty 5
Hike this 7.3-mile trail to the summit of Puzzle Mountain in Grafton Notch State Park near Newry. You'll ascend nearly 2,570 feet into the White Mountains of Maine through forest that has been protected from logging since the early twentieth century.

Gorham Mountain might only be 525 feet tall, but it's still a mountain.

Gorham Mountain Trail
Difficulty 2
Hike this 1.6-mile trail to the top of Gorham Mountain in Acadia National Park near Bar Harbor. This quick out-and-back trail will connect you to several other trails in the park, but will also give you great views of the surrounding park.

A view of Screw Auger Falls and its gorge.

Screw Auger Falls Trail
Difficulty 1
Hike this incredibly short .2-mile trail in Grafton Notch State Park near Newry to see the Screw Auger Falls along Bear River. Enjoy the falls and then take a walk up the river from stone to stone.

Looking out across Grafton Notch State Park from near the summit of Old Speck Mountain.

Old Speck Mountain Trail
Difficulty 5

Hike this 7.4-mile trail in Grafton Notch State Park near Newry to climb to the summit of Old Speck Mountain, Maine's fifth highest peak. You'll ascend 2,870 feet into the White Mountain's most northeastern range to the top of the range's most northeastern peak in America's most northeastern state.

Be sure to visit Thunder Hole during high tide to hear the wonder.

Thunder Hole to Sand Beach
Difficulty 2

Hike this 1.7-mile trail along the shores of the Atlantic Ocean in Acadia National Park near Bar Harbor. You'll start the trail near Thunder Hole, where high-tide water will shoot through the holes in the rocks, to Sand Beach where you can spend the afternoon soaking in the rays and water.

The terrain in the White Mountains can be absolutely magical with the right weather.

Rumford Whitecap Trail
Difficulty 4
Hike this 5.8-mile trail and ascend nearly 1,700 feet into the White Mountains of western Maine to summit Whitecap Mountain. The summit has several viewpoints to look out upon, so be sure to explore a bit when you reach the peak.

A photo of Jordan Pond with the Bubbles rock formation in the distance.

Jordan Pond Full Loop Trail
Difficulty 3
Hike this 3.1-mile trail in Acadia National Park on Mount Desert Island to meander through the woods along the shore of Jordan Pond. The rocky shoreline may have you watching your feet more than looking at the mountains that surround you. Take your time and enjoy yourself.

Maryland

Maryland is the forty-second largest state in the United States. Because of the state's variety of terrain, geography, and topography, it is sometimes called "America in Miniature." Sixteen of the state's twenty-three counties have coastline along Chesapeake Bay, and the entire state has nearly 4,000 miles of coast along the bay. Chesapeake Bay plays a significant role in Maryland's economy, transportation, and recreation. The coastal plains surrounding the Chesapeake as well as Delaware's barrier islands offer sandy beachsides and wetlands that are great for coastal hiking. The state's panhandle features several different regions, including the Appalachian Plateau and Ridge and Valley regions, the Piedmont Plateau, the Blue Ridge Mountains, and the Allegheny Mountains. Maryland is very forested, and the state is filled with mountains, valleys, coastlines, and scenic waterways that provide hikers with numerous opportunities to get outside.

The South Mountain State Park is home to several mountains to climb and features several waterfalls, including the 80-foot High Shoals Falls.

Appalachian Trail to Annapolis Rock
Difficulty 3
Hike 5.1 miles along the Appalachian Trail in South Mountain State Park near Boonsboro to climb nearly 800 feet to the Annapolis Rock overlook. You'll see Greenbrier Lake in the distance as well as Black Rock Cliff. Follow the white blazes until you reach the top, and then follow the blue blazes to reach Annapolis Rock.

The hike to Cascade Falls can be very muddy after it rains, so be sure to bring proper footwear.

Cascade Falls Loop Trail
Difficulty 2
Hike 2.3-miles on this loop trail through the Patapsco Valley State Park near Catonsville. You'll start your hike on the banks of the Patapsco River and then into the forest where you'll cross several streams before you reach Cascade Falls.

The Potomac River comprises the border between Maryland and Virginia, and Great Falls can be seen from either state.

Great Falls Overlook Loop
Difficulty 3
Hike this 5.8-mile loop in Chesapeake and Ohio Canal National Historic Park near Potomac where you will traverse a rocky trail along the Upper Potomac River. There is a section of the trail that is extremely rocky and can be difficult for some hikers.

The trail up to Wolf Rock and Chimney Rock is rocky, shaded, and verdant.

Wolf Rock & Chimney Rock Trail
Difficulty 3
Hike this 3.4-mile loop trail in Catoctin Mountain Park near Thurmont to see the interesting rock formations and the stands of old hardwoods and mountain laurels. This area is great for rock climbing and bouldering for those who are more adventurous.

McKeldin Switchback Trail
Difficulty 3

Hike this 3.9-mile trail in McKeldin Recreation Area near Marriottsville. You'll walk along the North Branch Patapsco River and see the river's rapids and several small waterfalls tumbling into the river.

Catoctin Mountain Extended Loop Trail
Difficulty 5

Hike this 9.9-mile loop trail in Catoctin Mountain Park near Thurmont to ascend nearly 1,700 feet to the summit of Catoctin Mountain. You'll pass several geologic formations like Cunningham Falls, Hog Rock, and Thurmont Vista along the way.

A view from the summit of Catoctin Mountain.

Swallow Falls State Park has hemlock trees that are nearly 300 years old, some of the oldest trees left in the state.

Swallow Falls Canyon Trail
Difficulty 1

Hike this short 1.1-mile hike in the Swallow Falls State Park near Oakland. Large hemlock trees tower above you to provide shade as you work your way toward the falls.

A view of the Potomac River from Weverton Cliffs.

Weverton Cliffs
Difficulty 2

Hike this 1.9-mile out-and-back trail in South Mountain State Park near Knoxville. Although you will only ascend about 600 feet, the trail starts with stone steps and then continues with switchbacks up to the steep cliffs. The trail can be very steep at points, but you will reach your destination quickly.

Rocks State Park covers a very rocky area of Maryland and provides opportunities for rock climbing and bouldering.

Falling Branch Trail
Difficulty 2

Hike this 1.3-mile trail in Rocks State Park near Pylesville to make your way to the Kilgore Falls. Kilgore Falls is Maryland's second tallest waterfall.

A view from the peak of Sugarloaf Mountain.

Northern Peaks Trail
Difficulty 5

Hike this 7.4-mile loop trail in Sugarloaf Mountain Natural Area near Dickerson to ascend nearly 1,500 feet to the top of Sugarloaf Mountain.

Massachusetts

Massachusetts is the forty-fourth largest state in the United States. The state's eastern border lies on the Atlantic Ocean, and its coastline is filled with large bays, including Massachusetts Bay, Buzzards Bay, Mount Hope Bay, and Cape Cod Bay. The southeastern coastline features Cape Cod, a large, sandy peninsula that stretches into the Atlantic Ocean. Just south of Cape Cod are the famously quaint islands of Martha's Vineyard and Nantucket. Central Massachusetts consists of flat agricultural plains that extend westward until the foothills of the Berkshire and Taconic Mountain Ranges. Western Massachusetts is mountainous and hilly and provides several areas for hikers to explore. Aside from the coastal regions, Massachusetts is home to several major waterways that are undergoing cleanup from centuries of industrial pollution that has decimated local fish populations. The state's highest point is Mount Greylock in the Taconic Mountains, standing at 3,491 feet above sea level.

Mount Holyoke Range State Park features a 7-mile long ridgeline following the mountains with streams, wetlands, and forests covering the park's lowlands.

Mount Norwottuck
Difficulty 3
Hike this 3.4-mile loop trail near Amherst in Mount Holyoke Range State Park to gain fantastic views of Pioneer Valley.

Skyline Trail
Difficulty 3
Hike this 3-mile loop trail in Blue Hills Reservation near Milton to see fantastic views of the Boston metropolitan area. If you want to climb more, you can go to the top of Eliot Tower.

Skyline Outer Reservoir Trail
Difficulty 4
Hike this 8.1-mile trail in Middlesex Fells Reservation near Medford. You'll ascend nearly 1,200 feet to get views of the Boston area.

Rock Circuit
Difficulty 4
Hike this 4.2-mile loop trail through Middlesex Fells Reservation near Medford and be prepared to climb over everything in sight. This trail seems to take the hardest way possible in this rocky landscape, so be prepared to climb.

Race Brook Falls & Mount Everett
Difficulty 5
Hike this 6.1-mile out-and-back trail in Mount Everett State Reservation near Sheffield and ascend nearly 2,200 feet to the summit of Mount Everett. This trail is rocky and steep, so be prepared for a workout to get to the top.

A hiker heading toward Mount Greylock in the distance.

Bellows Pipe Trail
Difficulty 5

Hike this 5.7-mile out-and-back trail in Mount Greylock State Reservation near Adams to climb to the peak of the state's highest mountain, Mount Greylock. You'll ascend nearly 2,200 feet, and on a clear day, it is said you can see nearly 90 miles away.

Boston Harbor Islands National Recreation Area features several trails to hike with grand views of downtown Boston.

World's End Trail
Difficulty 2

Hike this 3.8-mile trail in Boston Harbor Islands National Recreation Area near Hingham to explore the southern coastal regions of Boston Harbor. There are rolling hills and rocky shorelines, and every once in a while you'll get a glimpse of downtown Boston across the water.

Bash Bish Falls is a double cascade waterfall and falls nearly fifty-nine feet into the pool below. Swimming is not allowed.

Bash Bish Falls Trail
Difficulty 2

Hike this 2.1-mile out-and-back trail in Bash Bish Falls State Park to see magnificent falls which are the highest in the state. Nestled between Bash Bish Brook and the Taconic Mountains rising above you, this trail will take you to the serene falls at the end of the trail.

Watatic Mountain is a 1,800 foot mountain in north-central Massachusetts.

Wapack Trail
Difficulty 3

Hike this 2.8-mile trail in Watatic Mountain State Wildlife Area near Ashburnham. You'll climb to the top of Watatic Mountain and Nutting Hill along the way and gain views of where you started.

The trail in Monument Mountain Reservation will provide you views of the Housatonic River, the Taconic Mountains, and the Berkshire Mountains.

Hickey & Peeskawso Peak Trail
Difficulty 2

Hike this 2.4-mile loop trail in the Monument Mountain Reservation near Stockbridge to climb up to the top of Hickey and Peeskawso Peak. You'll pass by waterfalls over Melville's Tavern Cave and then to the summit. Be careful, the trail can be slick when wet.

Michigan

Michigan is the eleventh largest state in the United States. The state consists of two peninsulas surrounded by four of the five Great Lakes. Lake Michigan, Lake Superior, Lake Erie, and Lake Huron comprise most of the state's borders. Because the state is surrounded by the Great Lakes, it is the only state whose entire water system feeds into the Great Lakes-St. Lawrence Watershed. Michigan shares its southern border with Indiana and Ohio. The two peninsulas are separated from one another by the Straits of Mackinac. The Lower Peninsula of Michigan is much larger and much more populated than the Upper Peninsula. The Lower Peninsula is the shape of a mitten; the Thumb of the mitten is mostly flat with few hills, while the northern section of the Lower Peninsula consists of rolling hills and glacial moraines. The Upper Peninsula contains some of the oldest mountains in the world, the Porcupine Mountains, which rise as much as 2,000 feet above sea level. Nearly fifty percent of the state is still covered in forest, and the state is the largest state east of the Mississippi River. The territorial waters within the state are second in size only to Alaska, and offer Michiganders plenty of waterbound summertime activities to participate in.

Take the Chapel Loop in Pictured Rocks National Lakeshore to see Chapel Creek tumble into the deep waters of Lake Superior from Chapel Beach.

Chapel Loop
Difficulty 4

Hike this 10.2-mile loop trail in Pictured Rocks National Lakeshore in the Upper Peninsula near Munising to see the glorious Lake Superior shoreline through the dense forested stands of maple, beech, birch, and pine trees. This is truly a beautiful area along North America's largest lake.

The Manistee River winding through Manistee National Forest's red pines and northern hardwoods.

Manistee River Loop Trail
Difficulty 5

Hike this 21.7-mile loop trail through Manistee National Forest near Mesick in the Lower Peninsula. Start along the shore of Hodenpyl Dam Pond and work your way south along the Manistee River. This trail is perfect for backpacking or stopping along the way to fish.

Sugarloaf Mountain
Difficulty 2

Hike this 1.2-mile loop trail near Marquette in the Upper Peninsula for beautiful views and quiet forests. There is a bit of scrambling up rocks necessary, but that only adds to the fun on your way to the summit.

Penosha Trail
Difficulty 3

Hike this 5-mile trail in Brighton State Recreation Area near Brighton in the Lower Peninsula. Formed by glaciers several thousands of years ago, this area is filled with several steep rolling hills to explore.

The dunes along the Lake Michigan shoreline can be as tall as 500 feet.

Empire Bluff Trail
Difficulty 3

Hike this 1.5-mile trail in Sleeping Bear Dunes National Lakeshore near Empire in the Lower Peninsula. Climb high into the dunes and maple-beach forests on the shores of Lake Michigan to garner views of the tremendous coastal bluffs and dunes.

Miners Falls drops nearly forty feet.

Miners Falls Trail
Difficulty 2

Hike this 1.2-mile trail in Pictured Rocks National Lakeshore near Munising in the Upper Peninsula to see one of the lakeshore's several waterfalls. Once you reach the top of the waterfall follow the staircase down to a viewing platform.

A photo of Lake of the Clouds from the Escarpment Trail.

Escarpment Trail
Difficulty 5

Hike this 8.2-mile trail in Porcupine Mountains Wilderness State Park near Ontonagon in the Upper Peninsula. Follow the ridgeline in the mountains to the Lake in the Clouds, which is one of the area's most popular destinations.

A view from the Bird Hills Trail crossing the Barton Dam along the Huron River.

Bird Hills Trail
Difficulty 3

Hike this 4.8-mile trail in Bird Hills Nature Area in Ann Arbor in the Lower Peninsula. Along the way you'll cross the Huron River twice and walk through the shady forests.

A photo taken from the shore of Silver Lake along the Potawatomi Trail.

Potawatomi Trail
Difficulty 5

Hike this 17.4-mile trail in Pinckney Recreation Area near Pinckney in the Lower Peninsula. You'll hike through the wetlands surrounding this area to the shores of Silver Lake and Halfmoon Lake.

Lookout Point is about 0.6 miles from the trailhead.

Pyramid Point Loop
Difficulty 3

Hike this 2.8-mile loop trail through Sleeping Bear Dunes National Lakeshore to experience sweeping views of Lake Michigan. Walk through low pastures between dunes and then climb up into the maple-beech forests underlaid with sand.

Minnesota

Minnesota is the twelfth largest state in the United States, and is the second largest state east of the Mississippi River. Much of lower Minnesota consists of flat and semi-hilly pastures that were formed in the last glaciation nearly 12,000 years ago. The far southeast section of the state bordering Wisconsin is a part of the hilly Driftless Area that was untouched by the glaciation. Northern Minnesota is home to some of the oldest rocks on Earth, dating back nearly 3.6 billion years, which is about eighty percent of the Earth's age. Volcanic activity some two billion years ago deposited lava into the waters of northern Minnesota whose remnants today form the Canadian Shield rock formation and Iron Mountain Range. Minnesota is truly the "Land of 10,000 Lakes," and then some with an actual total of lakes near 11,800 that are at least ten acres in size. There are plenty of recreational activities in the state, from hiking into the mountains to walking along meandering rivers deep in one of the state's several forests.

These two falls at Devil's Kettle tumble over extremely ancient volcanic rock. The eastern falls (right) tumbles 50 feet over two ledges and then into the stream below. The western falls (left) falls into a pothole where the water just "disappears underground."

Devil's Kettle
Difficulty 2
Hike this 2-mile trail in Judge C.R. Magney State Park near East Cook in far northern Minnesota. You'll hike along Brule River toward the kettle and its majestic waterfalls.

While you're at Split Rock Lighthouse State Park, be sure to check out the Split Rock Lighthouse perched high above the stormy waters of Lake Superior.

Split Rock Ridge Trail
Difficulty 4
Hike this 7.7-mile section of the Superior Hiking Trail in Split Rock Lighthouse State Park near Beaver Bay in northern Minnesota. You'll walk along the Split Rock River and see the water tumble toward the shores of Lake Superior.

Although you're surrounded by the city of St. Paul, the Pike Island Trail feels remote along the banks of the Mississippi River.

Pike Island Loop
Difficulty 3
Hike this 3.9-mile loop trail in Fort Snelling State Park in St. Paul along the Mississippi River. Pike Island is nestled in the northern waters of the Mississippi, and the trail that leads you there is one of many trails the Minneapolis-St. Paul metropolitan area offers.

High Falls tumbles 120 feet into the pool below.

Tettegouche State Park Trail
Difficulty 1
Hike this 1.6-mile trail in Tettegouche State Park near Silver Bay in northern Minnesota. You'll hike to Baptism River where High Falls tumbles into the pool below.

The maple forests surrounding the Bean and Bear Lakes area exhibit beautiful colors in the fall.

Bean and Bear Lakes Trail
Difficulty 4
Hike this 6.3-mile section of the Superior Hiking Trail outside of Silver Bay in northern Minnesota. You'll ascend nearly 1,000 feet to make it up to the overlook. Great views of Bean and Bear Lakes await you.

Early explorers of the Midwest and First Nation peoples had difficulty with this section of the St. Louis River and had to divert their route to the Grand Portage of the Saint Louis River 7 miles away.

Silver Creek Trail
Difficulty 3
Hike this 3.4-mile loop trail in Jay Cooke State Park near Carlton. You'll travel along the 13-mile St. Louis River gorge to see unique rock formations and rushing waterscapes.

The Temperance River flowing through a gorge of igneous rock that was deposited in the region 1.1 billion years ago.

Temperance River Falls Loop
Difficulty 3
Hike this 3.3-mile trail in Temperance River State Park near Schroeder along the Temperance River. You'll hike through the pine forests before entering into the Temperance River gorge.

Fifth Falls is the uppermost and last waterfall on this trail, but it is also the smallest waterfall you'll see on the hike.

Fifth Falls & Superior Hiking Trail Loop
Difficulty 2
Hike this 3-mile trail in Gooseberry Falls State Park near Silver Creek Township to travel up the rocky Gooseberry River to its falls. You'll see fabulous rock formations, five waterfalls, and dense northern Minnesota forest.

Eagle Mountain is the highest point in Minnesota, and the Eagle Mountain Trail will take you right to the top.

Eagle Mountain Trail
Difficulty 3
Hike this 6.4-mile out-and-back trail in Superior National Forest near Grand Marais in northern Minnesota. You'll summit the 2,300 foot high Eagle Mountain, but you'll only need to ascend 650 feet yourself to get to the top. Views of the surrounding lakes and forest abound.

A view of Oberg Lake from Oberg Mountain. Oberg Mountain is part of the Sawtooth Range which features several rocky ridges and low mountains alongs the North Shore of Lake Superior.

Oberg Mountain Loop
Difficulty 3
Hike this 2.3-mile loop section of the Superior Hiking Trail in Superior National Forest near Tofte in northern Minnesota. You'll ascend just 500 feet to reach this summit, and along the way you'll have the opportunity to see the surrounding forest from several overlooks.

Mississippi

Mississippi is the thirty-second largest state in the United States. The entire state is a part of the Eastern Gulf Coastal Plain with low-lying hills like the state's Pine Hills, North Central Hills, and Fall Line Hills. The Mississippi River makes up most of the state's western border and the northwest portion of Mississippi is considered to be a part of the Mississippi Delta. To the south of the state, Mississippi does not technically share shoreline with the Gulf of Mexico but rather the Mississippi Sound. The southern shores of Mississippi are somewhat protected by a few barrier islands, including Petit Bois Island, Horn Island, East and West Ship Islands, and Deer Island. Biloxi Bay, Bay St. Louis, and Pascagoula Bay are all major topographical features along the shoreline. Several major rivers flow in the state aside from its namesake, the Mississippi River, including the Big Black, Pearl, Yazoo, and Pascagoula Rivers. Much of the western portion of the state is part of the Mississippi Alluvial Plain which consists of rich soil deposited by Mississippi floodwaters.

Longleaf Trace Trail
Difficulty 5
Hike, walk, run, or bike this 40.5-mile paved trail near Hattiesburg through several of the region's densely forested pockets.

Noxubee Hills Outer Loop
Difficulty 5
Hike or mountain bike this 26-mile trail in Tombigbee National Forest near Ackerman. You'll ascend nearly 1,900 feet through the rolling hills of the region.

One of the nearly fifty waterfalls in the Clark Creek Nature Area.

Clark Creek Primitive Trail
Difficulty 3
Hike this 4.3-mile loop trail in Clark Creek Natural Area near Woodville to see a waterfall tumbling deep in the Mississippi forests of pine, magnolia, and beech trees. There are several waterfalls in the area and this trail will take you to see a few.

Fontainebleau Nature Trail
Difficulty 1
Hike or walk this 1.6-mile trail in Mississippi Sandhill Crane National Wildlife Refuge near Ocean Springs along the Gulf Shore. Walk along the Davis Bayou and see the wetlands of the Deep South.

The Fontainebleau Trail takes a short trip through protected lands for nesting sandhill cranes.

The swinging bridge crossing Bear Creek in the Tishomingo State Park.

Bear Creek Outcropping Trail
Difficulty 2

Hike this 1.8-mile loop trail in Tishomingo State Park near Dennis. Walk along Bear Creek to see unique rock formations with their nooks and crevices filled with ferns. You'll also see a waterfall if you take the spur trail.

The De Soto National Forest along the Tuxachanie Trail is filled with ridges lined with pine trees and tea-colored streams.

Tuxachanie Trail
Difficulty 4

Hike this 12.9-mile out-and-back trail in De Soto National Forest near Saucier. Along the way, you'll pass by ponds and cross streams while you catch up on the area's history with the historic plaques posted along the trail.

Tishomingo State Park lies at the southern end of the Appalachian Mountains and offers rocky terrain to scramble and climb.

CCC Camp Trail Loop
Difficulty 2

Hike this 3.6-mile trail in Tishomingo State Park near Dennis. This trail is part of the Natchez Trace Trail and offers views of great rock formations along Bear Creek.

Dunn's Falls was created in the 1850s by an Irish immigrant named John Dunn to power the water wheel that is still in operation today.

Dunn's Falls Trail
Difficulty 1

Hike or walk this .4-mile trail near Enterprise to see Dunn's Falls and the old mill.

The Red Bluff Trail will take you to the shores of Pearl River as it winds through the terrain.

Red Bluff Trail
Difficulty 1

Hike or walk this .9-mile loop trail near Foxworth that will take you down to the Pearl River and train tracks.

The park surrounding Bonita Lake is nearly 33,000 acres and features several trails for hiking and running.

Bonita Lakes Trail
Difficulty 3

Hike this 7.6-mile loop trail near Meridian to travel along the shores of Bonita Lake.

Missouri

Missouri is the twenty-first largest state in the United States. The state has three distinct regions that give the "Show Me" State its rugged topography. The Ozark Plateau comprises most of southern Missouri south of the Missouri River to the Arkansas border. The area is filled with steep, rolling hills, seasonal creeks, dense oak forests, and the St. Francis Mountains. Missouri's southeastern bootheel is the state's second distinct geographic region in that it descends from the Ozark Plateau into the alluvial plain of the Mississippi River. The third major region of Missouri is the northern plains that are a part of the Interior Plains of North America. Despite its three distinct regions though, much of the state of Missouri is filled with undulating hills either intersected with rocky outcroppings and ridges or forested prairies. Much of the Ozark Plateau has been carved by erosion over the millenia, and caves in the dolomite and limestone bedrock are quite common. Missouri is home to the oak-hickory hardwood forests of Mark Twain National Forest, Missouri River, Marvel Cave, and Lake of the Ozarks, and it provides ample opportunities for outdoor fun.

Whispering Pines Trail
Difficulty 5

Hike this 11.3-mile trail in Hawn State Park near Farmington to pass over scenic ridges and through forests. There are beautiful rock formations and even some creek crossings so be sure to bring your hiking boots to explore.

Bell Mountain Loop Trail
Difficulty 5

Hike this 11.6-mile loop trail in Bell Mountain Wilderness near Belleview through the oak-hickory hardwood forests of the Ozark Plateau.

River Scene Trail Loop
Difficulty 2

Hike this 3.1-mile loop trail in Castlewood State Park near Ballwin to climb along the bluffs over the Meramec River and then into the river valley. You'll see a historic abandoned resort along the river and beautiful river views.

Castlewood State Park is just outside of the metropolitan area of St. Louis and is one of the area's best locations for mountain biking.

The Double Arch rock formation at Pickle Springs Natural Area.

Pickle Springs Natural Area
Difficulty 2

Hike this 1.9-mile trail in Pickle Springs Natural Area to see shady box canyons and the creeks that run through them. Along the way, you'll see shallow caves, seasonal waterfalls, and bluffs tucked away into the woods.

An icy winter at Paddy Creek Wilderness along the Big Piney Trail.

Big Piney Trail
Difficulty 5

Hike this 16.1-mile trail in Paddy Creek Wilderness near Roby in the Ozark Plateau to see seasonal waterfalls and rugged outcroppings of rocks. You'll ascend nearly 1,900 feet going up and down the bluffs and rolling hills of the region. There are several creek crossings along the way.

Elephant Rocks State Park is a great place for the family to go hiking, climbing, and exploring for the day.

Elephant Rocks Braille Trail
Difficulty 2

Hike this 1-mile loop trail in Elephant Rocks State Park near Pilot Knob in the Ozark Plateau.

This shady little creek lies at the base of Missouri's highest point, Taum Sauk Mountain at 1,765 feet above sea level.

Mine Sauk Falls Trail
Difficulty 3

Hike this 2.9-mile loop trail in Taum Sauk Mountain State Park near Ironton and go around the base of Taum Sauk Mountain to the low, tumbling Mine Sauk Falls. The trail is rocky and steep at points and may require scrambling, but the lookouts the climb provides are amazing.

Taum Sauk Mountain Trail just might be the easiest hike to a state's highest point in the nation.

Taum Sauk Mountain Trail
Difficulty 1

Hike this 1.9-mile out-and-back trail in Taum Sauk Mountain State Park near Arcadia to Missouri's highest point, Taum Sauk Mountain. You'll reach an altitude of 1,765 feet by only ascending 69 feet on this trail.

The shut-ins along the East Fork Black River in Johnson's Shut-Ins State Park.

Johnson's Shut-Ins State Park Trail
Difficulty 3

Hike this 2.4-mile trail in Johnson's Shut-Ins State Park near Lesterville to see the shut-ins rock formations along the East Fork Black River. You'll walk through the hardwood forests of the Ozark Plateau and through rocky sections along the river.

One of the many shallow shelter caves in Don Robinson State Park.

Sandstone Canyon Trail
Difficulty 3

Hike this 3.9-mile loop trail in Don Robinson State Park near Eureka to see some of the region's shallow caves, shady canyons, and dense forests.

Montana

Montana is the fourth largest state in the United States and is home to nearly one hundred different mountain ranges. The state is divided between eastern and western regions by the Continental Divide. A majority of the state's mountain ranges are in the western region of the state and almost all of those ranges are subranges of the Northern Rocky Mountains. Some of these ranges include the Beartooth, Absaroka, Bitterroot, Cabinet, and Sapphire Mountains. The Beartooth Plateau is the largest land mass above 10,000 feet in the United States, and it is also home to the state's highest point, Granite Peak at 12,799 feet above sea level. East of the Continental Divide, the Great Plains dominate nearly sixty percent of the state. The plains are less populated than the mountains of the west, but they have several smaller mountain ranges within them. Montana's largest growing sector is tourism with several popular destinations for people who enjoy the outdoors including Glacier National Park, Yellowstone National Park, Flathead Lake, and Big Sky Resort.

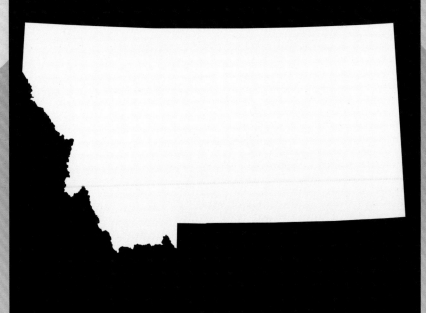

The hike to Wanless Lake is very difficult and is only recommended for experienced hikers. A camp is located about halfway through the trail.

Wanless Lake Trail
Difficulty 5

Hike this 19-mile out-and-back trail near Trout Creek to the shore of Wanless Lake high in Kaniksu National Forest. You'll ascend nearly 5,000 feet on this trail through the pine forests and along quaint streams.

Lava Lake with Spanish Peaks behind it.

Lava Lake Trail
Difficulty 4

Hike this 6-mile out-and-back trail in Custer Gallatin National Forest near Gallatin Gateway. Ascend nearly 1,600 feet to the shores of Lava Lake surrounded by the Spanish Peaks.

A shot from the summit of Storm Castle Peak.

Storm Castle Peak
Difficulty 5

Hike this 5.2-mile trail in Custer Gallatin National Forest near Bozeman to the summit of Storm Castle Peak. You'll ascend nearly 1,800 feet and the path gets awfully narrow at points along steep drops off.

Avalanche Lake is filled with the meltwater of Sperry Glacier in the mountains above.

Trail of the Cedars
Difficulty 3

Hike this 5.9-mile out-and-back trail in Glacier National Park near Lake McDonald to see one of Montana's most popular destinations. You'll hike to the shores of Lake Avalanche and see its famous crystal-clear blue waters.

Virginia Falls tumbles nearly fifty feet into the pool below.

St. Mary & Virginia Falls Trail
Difficulty 3
Hike this 2.9-mile trail in Glacier National Park near Siyeh Bend to see several waterfalls in a short distance. St. Mary and Virginia Falls both steal the show as they fall over thirty feet into their respective creeks.

The Yellowstone River is 700 miles long and is filled with meltwater from the snowy mountains above.

Artist Point
Difficulty 2
Hike this .2-mile trail in Yellowstone National Park near Gardiner to see spectacular views of Yellowstone's Grand Canyon. You'll see the Yellowstone River rushing and the Lower Falls too.

Hikers walking the Beehive Basin Trail No. 40.

Beehive Basin Trail No. 40
Difficulty 5
Hike this 7.1-mile trail near Big Sky to explore the prairies nestled between the mountains with great views of the Spanish Peaks above.

The hot waters from the springs in Yellowstone National Park deposit calcium carbonate and have built the Mammoth Terraces over thousands of years.

Mammoth Terraces & Upper Ter Loop
Difficulty 3
Hike this 3.6-mile loop trail in Yellowstone National Park near Gardiner to explore in this famous national park and its waterfalls. You'll see the hot springs and magnificent rock formations that are deposited and formed before your eyes.

Use caution when in Glacier National Park because grizzly bears are known to be in this area during the summer.

Hidden Lake Overlook
Difficulty 3
Hike this 2.9-mile trail in Glacier National Park near Siyeh Bend to see grasslands and mountains along the way. At the end of the trail, you'll look over Hidden Lake. Some parts of the trail are extremely steep and rocky.

Iceberg Lake Trail
Difficulty 5
Hike this 9.3-mile trail in Glacier National Park near Siyeh Bend to pass through open terrains and forest nooks before reaching Ptarmigan Falls. After the falls, you'll make your way to Iceberg Lake where you can hopefully see icebergs floating in the water.

Nebraska

Nebraska is the sixteenth largest state in the United States. It has two distinct regions, the Dissected Till Plains and the Great Plains. The Dissected Till Plains are found in the eastern portion of the state and are home to the state's two largest cities, Lincoln and Omaha. The till plains are mostly composed of gently rolling hills and forests. The Great Plains are much more flat and dry and compose most of the western part of the state. The Great Plains in this region are nearly treeless and stretch into eastern Colorado and Wyoming. The western part of the state also has several distinct ecosystems within the Great Plains, including the Sandhill, Pine Ridge, Rainwater Basin, High Plains, and Wildcat Hills regions. Three major rivers run the length of the state from west to east, including the Platte, Niobrara, and Republican Rivers. The National Forest Service operates the Nebraska National Forest, the Oglala National Grassland, and the Samuel R. McKelvie National Forest. Most of Nebraska falls within Tornado Alley and the state experiences severe thunderstorms and tornadoes in the spring and summer.

Rock Bluff Trail Loop
Difficulty 4
Hike this 5.9-mile trail in Indian Cave State Park near Falls City and ascend nearly 1,115 feet along the rolling hills on the banks of the Missouri River.

Schramm Park Nature Loop
Difficulty 1
Hike this 2-mile trail in Schramm Park State Recreation Area near Gretna through the riparian forests lining the northern shores of the Platte River. Follow the trail markers because there are several spur trails that can lead you off course.

The stairway leads to the mouth of Indian Cave in Indian Cave State Park.

The Oglala National Grassland is home to badland terrain where the Toadstool rock formations can be found.

Indian Cave Trail
Difficulty 3
Hike this 3.1-mile trail in Indian Cave State Park near Falls City to see the great bluffs surrounding the Missouri River. Indian Cave can be reached by crossing a bridge, but there are times when the bridge is out of service.

Toadstool Trail
Difficulty 1
Hike this .8-mile trail in Oglala National Grassland near Harrison to see the beautiful grasslands nestled in western Nebraska's Great Plains.

A tumbling waterfall along the Platte River in Platte River State Park.

Platte River State Park Trail Loop
Difficulty 3

Hike this 6.7-mile loop trail in Platte River State Park near South Bend to walk along the banks of the Platte River. You'll cruise up and down the rolling hills and also see a tiny waterfall along the way.

A hiker heading toward Mount Greylock in the distance.

Standing Bear Lake Loop
Difficulty 2

Hike, walk, run, or bike this 3-mile trail in Standing Bear Lake Park to experience a quaint afternoon in Omaha. There are opportunities for picnicking, fishing, biking, and no-wake boating.

A wooded boardwalk leads the way through the forest in the Fontenelle Forest Nature Center.

Hickory & Ridge Trail Loop
Difficulty 2

Hike, walk, or run this 2.2-mile trail in Fontenelle Forest Nature Center near St. Columbans. This is a great walk near the Omaha metro-area, and the Fontenelle Nature Association manages nearly 2,000 acres of forest with 26 miles of marked trails.

Flanagan Lake is a man-made lake to help prevent flooding in Omaha.

Flanagan Lake Trail
Difficulty 3

Hike, walk, or run this 5.2-mile trail near Elkhorn to enjoy a leisurely afternoon along Lake Flanagan. This trail has several benches along the way to stop and enjoy the views.

Wehrspann Lake Full Loop Trail is open all year and can be a great place to explore during the winter.

Wehrspann Lake Full Loop
Difficulty 3

Hike this 6-mile trail through Chalco Hills Recreation Area around the perimeter of Wehrspann Lake. You'll go up and down the rolling hills along the lake.

The rugged bluffs and badlands of Scotts Bluff National Monument are a wondrous part of the varied ecology surrounding the Platte River.

Saddle Rock Trail
Difficulty 3

Hike this 3-mile trail in Scotts Bluff National Monument near Gering to walk through the arid plains of western Nebraska. You'll walk through the grasslands of spiderwort and through the foot tunnel that was built prior to Summit Road's vehicular tunnel.

Nevada

Nevada is the seventh largest state in the United States. It is the nineteenth least populated state in the United States and nearly three-quarters of its entire population live in the Las Vegas-Paradise metropolitan area. Much of the state can be characterized as a Basin and Range Province that has several north-to-south running mountain ranges with valleys between them. Many of these valleys collect water from the mountains below but do not have water outflows, so much of the water collected in these valleys form seasonal lakes. The mountain ranges of Nevada create "sky islands" of lush forest above the dry valleys below that allow for unique ecosystems to form high above sea level. There are several mountain peaks in the state that reach 13,000 feet, and most of the valleys in the state lie above 3,000 feet. Nevada is the driest state in the United States, and it has the second-highest number of mountains within its borders after Alaska.

Take a second to rest at the end of Hunter Creek Trail and put your feet in the icy water at the base of the waterfall.

Hunter Creek Trail
Difficulty 4
Hike this 6.4-mile trail in Humboldt-Toiyabe National Forest near Reno. You'll ascend nearly 1,240 feet to see the thirty-foot waterfall that is at the end of the rocky trail.

Scrambling the red sandstone might be necessary to reach the Calico Tanks in Red Rock Canyon Conservation Area.

Calico Tanks Trail
Difficulty 3

Hike this 2.2-mile hike in Red Rock Canyon National Conservation Area near Las Vegas to see beautiful sandstone formations and distant views of Las Vegas. You'll only ascend about 420 feet to reach these rock formations that you can explore and scramble for a fun afternoon.

Blocks of Aztec Sandstone at the abandoned Excelsior Sandstone Quarry along Turtlehead Peak Trail. The mine was in operation between 1905 and 1912.

Turtlehead Peak Trail
Difficulty 5

Hike this 4.6-mile trail in Red Rock Canyon Conservation Area near Blue Diamond to see ancient petroglyphs and an old sandstone quarry. You'll ascend nearly 1,988 feet to the sandy summit of Turtlehead Peak.

A view of the Spring Mountains from the Mary Jane Falls Trail trailhead.

Mary Jane Falls Trail
Difficulty 3

Hike this 3.9-mile trail in Mount Charleston Wilderness near Mount Charleston to ascend nearly 1,135 feet to the waterfall in Kyle Canyon. The Spring Mountains offer a great retreat for those looking to escape Las Vegas for a day.

A view of Mount Rose from Tahoe Rim Trail.

Mount Rose Trail
Difficulty 5

Hike this 10.7-mile trail in Mount Rose Wilderness near Incline Village and Crystal Bay to ascend nearly 2,395 feet to the summit of Mount Rose. You'll reach 10,778 feet above sea level on this trail and the views of the desert below are magnificent.

A view of Cathedral Rock and Echo Cliffs, which drop 1,000 feet to the valley floor below.

Cathedral Rock Trail
Difficulty 4

Hike this 2.8-mile trail in Humboldt-Toiyabe National Forest near Las Vegas to ascend nearly 1,000 feet to the 8,603 foot summit of Cathedral Rock. You'll pass Echo Cliffs through aspen and pine forests and then climb up the switchbacks to the rock's summit.

A waterfall situated along the banks of the Colorado River.

Gold Strike Hot Springs Trail
Difficulty 4

Hike this 6-mile trail in Lake Mead National Recreation Area near Boulder City in southern Nevada to visit the beautiful hot springs situated along the Colorado River. You'll ascend nearly 1,400 feet to visit several hot springs on the trail, and you'll use several sections of fixed rope to climb to the end of the trail.

The Van Sickle Bi-State Park straddles the borders of Nevada and California near Lake Tahoe.

Van Sickle Rim Trail
Difficulty 5

Hike this 8.1-mile trail in Van Sickle Bi-State Park near Stateline to ascend nearly 1,360 feet into the wilderness surrounding Lake Tahoe.

The Valley of Fire State Park is filled with beautiful formations of Aztec Sandstone which was deposited by 150-million-year-old sand dunes.

Fire Waves, White Domes & Seven Wonders Loop
Difficulty 3

Hike this 3.2-mile trail in Valley of Fire State Park near Overton to see the beautiful red sandstone rock formations of the Nevada desert. You'll pass the Fire Waves and White Domes rock formations along with several slot canyons that are worth exploring if you feel adventurous.

The Spring Mountains are home to several natural springs and several mountain peaks including Griffith and Bonanza Peak and Mount Wilson and Mount Potosi.

South Loop Trail
Difficulty 5

Hike this 10.2-mile trail in Spring Mountains National Recreation Area near Mount Charleston to ascend nearly 3,500 feet to summit Griffith Peak. The climb begins with your first step, but the strain and effort are paid back in full with the 360 degree views from the summit.

New Hampshire

New Hampshire is the forty-sixth largest state in the United States and is the tenth least populous state. It is one of six states that compose the United States' New England region in the northeastern part of the country. Despite the state's size, there are several distinct regions within New Hampshire, including the Great North Woods, the White Mountains, the Lake Region, the Merrimack Valley, the Seacoast, and others. The state has the shortest ocean coastline in the United States, measuring only eighteen miles along the Atlantic Ocean. The Great North Woods occupy the northern third of the state and the White Mountains are just south of it. The world's second-highest wind speed was recorded in the White Mountains at Mount Washington, with winds blowing at 231 miles per hour. The top of Mount Washington is known to have tornado-scale winds at least every three days, and there have been numerous deaths on the mountain due to wind speeds. The southern regions of the state are a bit flatter than the mountains of northern New Hampshire. It is home to the Merrimack River, an important feature in both New Hampshire and Massachusetts. Much of the state is still covered in forest like the New England acadian forests of the White Mountains and the Northeastern coastal forests found in the southern part of the state.

North Hampton Beach State Park is open all year around, but the winter weather in the area can make the beach a difficult place to visit.

Little Boar's Head Scenic Walk
Difficulty 2
Hike this 2.9-mile trail in North Hampton State Beach near Rye Beach to experience a small stretch of New Hampshire's extremely short Atlantic Coastline. Start next to Little River Swamp and see the wetlands and beach on this family-friendly trail.

A photo of Stairs Falls in the Franconia Notch State Park.

Mount LaFayette & Franconia Ridge Trail Loop
Difficulty 5
Hike this 8.4-mile loop in Franconia Notch State Park near Lincoln to ascend nearly 3,800 feet into the White Mountains and summit three peaks along the way. You climb to the tops of Little Haystack Mountain, Mount Lincoln, and Mount Lafayette as well as past Stairs Falls and Cloudland Falls.

Flume Gorge is located at the base of Mount Lincoln and was discovered in 1808 by a ninety-three-year-old woman while fishing. She had to convince her family the place was true, because it sounded unbelievable. The gorge truly is unbelievable.

Flume Gorge Trail
Difficulty 2
Hike this 2.2-mile trail in Franconia Notch State Park near Lincoln to walk into the beautifully rocky and steep Flume Gorge. The walls of granite tower nearly 90 feet above you at points while the creek tumbles just below your feet under the boardwalk.

A dog trotting along at the top of Mount Pemigewasset. Be careful at the top because there are drop offs from the ledge.

Indian Head Trail
Difficulty 4
Hike this 3.5-mile out-and-back trail in White Mountain National Forest near Lincoln to ascend nearly 1,525 feet to the summit of Mount Pemigewasset. At the top, you find yourself atop a huge granite rock face with great views of the White Mountains stretching before you.

The waves crashing upon Ragged Neck in Rye Harbor State Park.

Ragged Neck Trail
Difficulty 1
Hike this 1-mile trail in Rye Harbor State Park near Rye to walk out along the the rocky harbor, called the Ragged Neck. From the coast you can see the Isles of Shoals, a series of small islands 6 miles off the shore from New Hampshire and Maine.

A view of the Saco River from the Mount Willard Trail.

Mount Willard Trail
Difficulty 3
Hike this 3.1-mile trail in Crawford Notch State Park near Bretton Woods to ascend nearly 1,000 feet, pass a waterfall, and summit Mount Willard. This trail is very steep at points, but the views of the White Mountains, the Saco River Valley, and Crawford Notch from the top can't be beat.

A photo from the lookout tower on the top of Cannon Mountain in Franconia Notch State Park.

Lonesome Lake Trail
Difficulty 3
Hike this 3.1-mile trail in Franconia Notch State Park near Lincoln to reach the shores of Lonesome Lake. You ascend nearly 1,000 feet over rock slabs and stair sections to the top of Cannon Mountain and then to the beautiful lake in the high wilderness.

The rock slab sections of the Welch-Dickey Loop Trail can be difficult to traverse between November and May due to ice and snow in the area.

Welch-Dickey Loop Trail
Difficulty 4
Hike this 4.4-mile trail in White Mountain National Forest near Thornton to ascend nearly 1,700 feet into the forest to see great views of the Waterville Valley. Cross over large rock slabs, summit Welch and Dickey Mountains, and then begin your descent back.

The Sandwich Range in the White Mountains.

Hancock Trail
Difficulty 5
Hike this 9.1-mile trail in White Mountain National Forest near Lincoln and ascend nearly 2,600 feet into the White Mountains to the summit of Mount Hancock. The last mile of the hike to the top of Mount Hancock can be extremely difficult and may require you to scramble up large rock slabs.

There is plenty of water during the fall season for Champney Falls to flow in White Mountain National Forest.

Champney Falls Trail
Difficulty 2
Hike this 3.1-mile trail in White Mountain National Forest near Albany to follow along Champney Brook to Champney Falls. The falls cascade nearly seventy feet along the brook, but it can be underwhelming during dry seasons.

New Jersey

New Jersey is the forty-seventh largest state in the United States, and ranks eleventh in terms of its population size. Due to its relatively large population and small area, New Jersey ranks first in terms of population density among the fifty states. The state's eastern border is mostly composed of the Atlantic Ocean and its seaways. The Hudson River separates northern New Jersey from the New York boroughs of the Bronx and Manhattan, while Staten Island is separated from Jersey by the tidal strait of Kill van Kull. Southern New Jersey is composed of the Atlantic Coastal Plain, which is relatively flat with some rolling hills. As you move north, you rise in elevation into the Piedmont Plateau, the Highlands, and Valley and Ridge topographies of the Appalachian Mountains. The northwestern corner of New Jersey is home to the Kittatinny Mountains and the Delaware Water Gap. There are several major rivers in the state, including the Manasquan, Mullica, and Maurice Rivers. New Jersey has nearly 130-miles of coastline along the Atlantic Ocean, and much of the outer coastal plain in the state remains undeveloped due to the region's agricultural unsuitability. It is here that we can find the rich ecosystem of the Pine Barrens in New Jersey, filled with interior wetlands, bogs, and pine stands.

Pass this beautiful waterfall before you summit Schooley's Mountain.

Overlooking the Hudson River from the cliffsides inside Palisades Interstate Park.

The trail to the top of Wawayanda Mountain is covered with boulders and requires some strenuous climbing.

Schooley's Mountain Boulder Gorge Loop Trail
Difficulty 3
Hike this 3.1-mile trail in Schooley's Mountain Park near Long Valley. Like many of the hikes in New Jersey, this trail is rocky and filled with boulders.

White Shore & Long Path Loop Trail
Difficulty 3
Hike this 4.1-mile loop trail in Palisades Interstate Park near Alpine to hike along the Hudson River. You'll see a waterfall exiting into the Hudson and climb the Giant Stairs, a portion of the trail covered in boulders.

Stairway to Heaven
Difficulty 2
Hike this 2.6-mile trail in Wawayanda State Park near Vernon Township to the top of Wawayanda Mountain along the Appalachian Trail. From the end of the trail you'll see Vernon Valley, Pochuck Mountain, the Kittatinny and Catskill Mountains, and the Black Dirt Region of northwestern New Jersey.

A photo of the Lamington River in Black River County Park.

Black River Trail Loop
Difficulty 3

Hike this 6.4-mile trail in Black River County Park near Chester to walk the banks of the Lamington River.

The quiet and rocky shores of Ramapo Lake in Ramapo Mountain State Forest.

Ramapo Park Lake Loop
Difficulty 3

Hike this 6.6-mile trail in Ramapo Mountain State Forest near Oakland to hike to the shores of Ramapo Lake. Some of this trail is paved and although the trail may be long, there is little elevation gain along the way.

Follow the Mount Tammany Loop to scramble up steep rocky faces to see the famous Delaware Water Gap.

Mount Tammany Loop
Difficulty 3

Hike this 3.6-mile trail in Worthington State Forest near Pahaquarry to ascend nearly 1,200 feet to the summit of Mount Tammany. Follow the red and blue dot blazes to follow the trail through and see the Delaware Water Gap and the Delaware River.

A view of High Point from the High Point State Park.

Monument Trail Loop
Difficulty 2

Hike this 3.5-mile trail loop in High Point State Park near Wantage to hike to the highest point in the state. High Point is 1,795 feet above sea level, but you only need to ascend nearly 500 feet to get there.

Buttermilk Falls tumbles gently down the rocks of Flat Brook to create a beautiful cascade.

Buttermilk Falls & Crater Lake Loop Trail
Difficulty 5

Hike this 6.8-mile trail in Delaware Water Gap National Recreation Area near Newton to explore the woods, cross streams, and enjoy Buttermilk Falls. You walk the shores of Crater Lake and then Hemlock Pond and pass ridgelines into shady valleys.

Hemlock Falls Trail
Difficulty 4

Hike this 5.8-mile trail in South Mountain Reservation near Millburn to travel along several streams and up some inclines to the quaint waterfalls hidden in the deep woods of northeastern New Jersey.

Watchung Reservation History Trail
Difficulty 3

Hike this 6.3-mile trail in Watchung Reservation near Mountainside. You'll follow along the shady and quiet Blue Brook and toward its reservoir.

New Mexico

New Mexico is the fifth largest state in the United States and is home to the oldest capital in the United States, Santa Fe. Santa Fe was founded by the Spanish Empire in 1610 as the capital city of Nuevo Mexico in New Spain. The state varies in climate from alpine mountaintops and high-desert pine forests in the north and east of the state to low-lying deserts and the Rio Grande Valley in the south and west of the state. Northern New Mexico is dominated by the Colorado Plateau, which features rugged volcanic rock formations and the alpine mountains of the Sangre de Cristo Mountains, a southern range of the Rocky Mountains. Eastern New Mexico is still a part of the Great Plains and is covered in expansive grasslands. The southern portion of the state is a part of North America's largest desert, the Chihuahuan Desert, which is characterized by its long basins interspersed with mountains. Several of these mountains create "sky islands" at high elevations that have high amounts of moisture and biodiversity compared to the arid deserts below. New Mexico is home to the Rio Grande River, the fourth longest river in the United States, which creates a valley through almost the entirety of the state from north to south with lush riparian habitats that have supported human civilization for thousands of years.

The Santa Fe National Forest is one of many forests that still cover nearly one-third of the entire state of New Mexico.

Nambe Lake Trail
Difficulty 5
Hike this 6.9-mile trail in Santa Fe National Forest near Santa Fe to ascend nearly 2,000 feet into the Sangre de Cristo Mountains. The lake at the top might be underwhelming to some fresh water lovers but the effort it took to reach it is the real prize.

A photo of Wheeler Wilderness below Williams Lake Trail.

Williams Lake Trail
Difficulty 5
Hike this 8.5-mile out-and-back trail in Wheeler Peak Wilderness near Taos Ski Valley to ascend nearly 2,900 to the top of Wheeler Peak. You'll start off in the shady pine forests at the base of this mountain and then pass the treeline into windy alpine elevations. Start early and beware of afternoon storms atop this 13,163 foot peak.

A view from Organ Needles Peak at nearly 8,885 feet above sea level in Organ Mountain-Desert Peaks National Monument.

Organ Needles Trail
Difficulty 5
Hike this 5.8-mile hike in Organ Mountain-Desert Peaks National Monument near Organ to ascend nearly 3,500 feet into the beautiful and rocky Organ Mountains. You'll scramble up to Juniper Saddle, through Dark Canyon, and then to the summit of Needles Peak at 8,885 feet above sea level.

Dripping Springs is just that, a fresh water spring dripping over a small rock formation in Organ Mountain-Desert Peaks National Monument.

Dripping Springs Trail
Difficulty 2
Hike this 3-mile trail in Organ Mountain-Desert Peaks National Monument near Organ to hike through Desert Valley to see the Dripping Springs Waterfall.

Hike along the base of the Organ Mountains through the sagebrush and yucca foothills to the higher-elevation pine tree slopes.

Pine Tree Trail
Difficulty 3
Hike this 4-mile trail in Organ Mountain-Desert Peaks National Monument near Las Cruces to take in the beauty of the area's high-desert pine forests.

Lincoln National Forest offers 1,000,000 acres of pine and fir forests with several sub-alpine grasslands.

Osha Trail
Difficulty 2
Hike this 2.5-mile loop trail in Lincoln National Forest near Cloudcroft to walk through fir forests with views of the White Dunes.

Views of Santa Fe from atop Atalaya Mountain.

Atalaya Mountain Trail
Difficulty 5
Hike this 6.2-mile trail in Santa Fe National Forest near Santa Fe to ascend nearly 1,800 feet to the summit of Atalaya Mountain. You'll get exquisite views of Santa Fe and the surrounding mountains from the top of this 9,118 foot peak.

A photo of the La Luz & Crest Spur Loop Trail along the Sandia Crest.

La Luz & Crest Spur Loop
Difficulty 3
Hike this 4.6-mile trail in Cibola National Forest near Cedar Crest to walk along the Sandia Mountains' towering cliffs over Albuquerque. You'll ascend just 900 feet to walk a narrow path next to steep dropoffs that provide beautiful views.

A view of Albuquerque from the Sandia Mountains.

South Piedra Lisa Trail
Difficulty 4

Hike this 4.4-mile trail in Sandia Mountain Wilderness near Albuquerque to ascend nearly 1,300 feet into the wilderness to get away from the city for a bit. There is a huge outcropping of rocks at the end of the trail to get some views of the surrounding area.

A trail marker along the Alkali Flat Trail, which could easily be rendered invisible in the shifting dunes.

Alkali Flat Trail
Difficulty 3

Hike this 4.8-mile loop in White Sands National Park near Holloman Air Force Base to the dried shores of the disappearing Lake Otero. You'll walk up and down the white sand dunes that are not as easy to traverse as you'd think.

New York

New York is the twenty-seventh largest state in the United States. It is home to terrain that ranges from the low-lying coastal plains of Long Island and Manhattan to the rolling mountains of the Allegheny Plateau and the Catskill Mountains. Upstate New York comprises most of the state from the Catskill Mountains northward and contains many natural features including the Adirondack Mountains, Erie Canal, Lake Champlain, Otsego Lake, Oneida Lake, and the Delaware, Mohawk, and Susquehanna Rivers. From south to north there are three major mountainous regions in the state: the Appalachian Mountains in the south, the Catskills in the center, and the Adirondacks in the far north. The northern border of the state is composed of the St. Lawrence River which connects the east coast to the interior of the Midwestern United States via the Great Lakes. A part of this border is also composed of the Lake Ontario and Lake Erie shorelines, which flow into each other by the Niagara River, home of the Niagara Falls. The New York City metropolitan area is located on the state's southeastern border on one of the world's largest natural harbors and spans across Staten Island, Manhattan Island, and some of Long Island. New York City is the most populous city in the United States as a home to over 8 million people across its five boroughs. Aside from all of the attractions New York City provides, the state of New York has just as much to offer for outdoor enthusiasts.

Nearly every mile of Gertrude's Nose Trail offers awesome views of the surrounding Catskill Mountains.

Gertrude's Nose Trail
Difficulty 4
Hike this 6.9-mile trail in Minnewaska State Park Reserve near High Falls to climb nearly 1,100 feet through dense forests, past Millbrook Mountain, to the Gertrude's Nose overhang. Pass by cliffsides and rock formations and then take in the views from the precarious Gertrude's Nose rock formation at the end of this loop trail.

A photo of the view from the summit of Cascade Mountain.

Cascade Mountain Trail
Difficulty 5

Hike this 5.6-mile out-and-back trail in High Peaks Wilderness near Keene and ascend nearly 2,200 feet into the Adirondack Mountains. You'll summit both Cascade and Porter Mountains on this trail where you'll scramble up rock faces to the peak.

A photo of clouds creeping over the Catskill Mountains near Overlook Mountain Wild Forest.

Overlook Mountain Trail
Difficulty 4

Hike this 4.6-mile out-and-back trail in Overlook Mountain Wild Forest near Woodstock to ascend nearly 1,300 feet into the Catskill Mountains. You'll walk an old gravel road to the top where you can scope the Hudson River Valley below.

A photo of the Bear Mountain Bridge across the Hudson River taken from the top of Bear Mountain.

Bear Mountain Loop Trail
Difficulty 5

Hike this 3.8-mile trail in Bear Mountain State Park near Bear Mountain in the Hudson River Valley to climb to the top of Bear Mountain and the Perkins Memorial Tower. Begin the hike on the shores of Hessian Lake and then make the near 1,100-foot ascent out of the valley along the rocky trail.

A view of Ausable Lake from Indian Head Overlook in the High Peaks region of the Adirondack Mountains.

Indian Head & Rainbow Falls Trail
Difficulty 5

Hike this 10.8-mile loop trail in Adirondack Mountain Reserve near Keene to ascend nearly 2,000 feet to see several waterfalls, including Rainbow Falls. At the end of the trail is Indian Head, a rocky overhang looking over Ausable Lake.

Out of the nineteen waterfalls you'll see in Watkins Glen State Park, Cavern Cascade is the largest.

Indians, Finger Lakes, & Gorge Trail Loop
Difficulty 2
Hike this 2.6-mile loop trail in Watkins Glen State Park near Watkins Glen to walk along Glen's Stream and see the nineteen waterfalls along the way. After Glen Creek you'll enter into Cavern Cascade's deep and shaded gorge.

The hike up Bull Hill is rocky, but there is plenty of shade to protect you from the sun.

Bull Hill Loop
Difficulty 4
Hike this 5.4-mile trail in Hudson Highlands State Park Preserve near Cold Spring along the Hudson River. The trail can be steep at points and may require you to scramble up large slabs of rock to the top of Bull Hill.

A photo of the beautiful cascading falls along Enfield Creek in the Robert H. Treman State Park.

Rim Trail & Gorge Trail Loop
Difficulty 3

Hike this 4.3-mile trail in Robert H. Treman State Park near Newfield to walk along Enfield Creek's gorge and then circle back to walk along the ridge above the gorge. You'll see fantastic waterfalls and rock formations on this rocky trail, but swimming in the water is not allowed.

A view of Phelps Mountain, Mount Marcy, and Mount Colden from the shores of Mount Marcy Dam Pond in the High Peaks Wilderness.

Van Hoevenberg Trail
Difficulty 5

Hike this 16.7-mile out-and-back trail in the High Peaks Wilderness of the Adirondack Mountains near Lake Placid to ascend nearly 3,500 feet into the mountainous wilderness. You summit Mount Marcy at 5,184 feet above sea level.

A hiker getting comfy along the precarious Great Ledge atop Panther Mountain.

Giant Ledge & Panther Mountain Trail
Difficulty 5

Hike this 7.1-mile trail in Slide Mountain Wilderness near Big Indian to ascend nearly 2,000 feet into the Catskill Mountains. At the top of Panther Mountain, walk to the edge of Great Ledge to live life on the wild side, but please be careful.

North Carolina

North Carolina is the twenty-eighth largest state in the United States and is the ninth most populous of the fifty states. North Carolina has three distinct regions: the eastern Atlantic Coastal Plain, the central Piedmont Plateau, and the western Appalachian Mountains. The Appalachian Mountains are separated into four different sub-ranges, including the Great Smoky Mountains, the Blue Ridge Mountains, the Black Mountains, and the Brushy Mountains. The Smoky Mountains are the highest and longest range in the state and range in elevations from 3,000 feet above sea level to 6,000 feet. Mount Mitchell is the highest point in the state at 6,684 feet above sea level, and is also the highest point east of the Mississippi River. The Piedmont Plateau in central North Carolina is filled with forested rolling hills and the sprawling cities of Charlotte and Raleigh. In the Piedmont Plateau, you can find the Uwharrie Mountains, which are North Carolina's lowest lying mountain range, with an average elevation of 500 feet above sea level. Much of North Carolina is composed of the Atlantic Coastal Plain, which lies east of the Fall Line, an escarpment that separates the Coastal Plain from the Piedmont Plateau to the west. The soil of this coastal plain is sandy and sedimentary compared to the igneous rocks of the western hills and mountains. Along the coast of North Carolina lie the Outer Banks, which are a string of shifting islands. Due to the Outer Banks, much of mainland North Carolina's coast is swampy and harborless.

Crabtree Falls Trail
Difficulty 2
Hike this 2.6-mile loop trail along the Blue Ridge Parkway near Little Switzerland to see the gently tumbling falls along Big Crabtree Creek.

Hawksbill Mountain Trail
Difficulty 2
Hike this 2.4-mile trail in Linville Gorge Wilderness near Jonas Ridge to hike to a craggy ridge with beautiful views of the Appalachian Mountains. You'll see Linville Gorge nearly 2,000 feet below you and Jonas Ridge across the way.

The magnificent Looking Glass Rock peeking out of the smoke-like clouds.

A view from top of Mount Mitchell, the highest peak east of the Mississippi.

Looking Glass Rock Trail
Difficulty 5
Hike this 5.8-mile trail in Pisgah National Forest near Brevard to ascend nearly 1,700 feet into the Blue Ridge Mountains. This trail is named after the gigantic reflective rock walls you pass along the way to the top of the mountain.

Mount Mitchell Trail
Difficulty 5
Hike this 11.9-mile trail in the Pisgah National Forest near Montreat to ascend nearly 3,600 feet to the highest point in not only North Carolina but the highest point east of the Mississippi River. From the top of Mount Mitchell, you will see the surrounding Pisgah National Forest as well as Grandfather and Table Rocks.

A hiker climbing up Catawba Falls. Use caution if you decide to follow their example.

Catawba Falls Trail
Difficulty 2
Hike this 2.3-mile trail in Pisgah National Forest near Black Mountain to visit Catawba Falls. Beware of the waterfall's slick rocks. There have been multiple incidents of people falling and injuring themselves.

Here we see Rainbow Falls gushing after a recent rainstorm.

Rainbow Falls & Turtleback Falls Trail
Difficulty 3
Hike this 3.9-mile trail in Gorges State Park near Sapphire to see some of the state's most beautiful waterfalls. Walk along the banks of Horsepasture River to see not only Rainbow and Turtleneck Falls but two others along the way.

The Cape Hatteras Lighthouse is a beacon of safety along the Outer Banks, which have been called the "Graveyard of the Atlantic."

Buxton Woods Trail
Difficulty 1
Hike this .8-mile trail in Cape Hatteras National Seashore near Buxton in the Outer Banks of the Atlantic Coast. You'll walk through pine-tree forests, along sandy ridges, and over swampy wetlands. This area is also home to the famous Cape Hatteras Lighthouse.

Triple Falls might look like three distinct falls, but they are considered one waterfall.

Triple Falls Trail
Difficulty 2
Hike this 2.9-mile trail in DuPont State Recreational Forest near Henderson to walk the banks of Little River. You'll see Triple Falls, which falls nearly 125 feet.

Clingmans Dome Observation Tower is the highest point in the Smoky Mountains.

Clingmans Dome Observation Tower Trail
Difficulty 1
Hike this 1.2-mile trail in Great Smoky Mountains National Park near Bryson City to climb high into the Smoky Mountains by only ascending 300 feet. At the top of this modern observation tower, you'll get a panoramic view of the Smoky Mountains below you.

One of the several "chimneys" in the Linville Gorge State Park.

The Chimneys via Mountains-to-Sea Trail
Difficulty 2
Hike this 1.7-mile trail in Linville Gorge Wilderness near Jonas Ridge to see the rocky outcroppings along Jonas Ridge. You'll ascend nearly 300 feet along the ridge-line where you can climb, boulder, and scramble the rock formations.

North Dakota

North Dakota is the nineteenth largest state in the United States and is the fourth least populated state. It consists of three distinct regions: the Red River Valley along the state's eastern border with Minnesota, the central Missouri Plateau and Drift Prairie, and the Great Plains of the west. The Red River Valley is the remnant of the ancient Lake Agassiz, which was filled with glacial meltwater from the last glaciation. The area today is a fertile, lush, and flat valley used agriculturally to grow wheat, sugarbeet, and corn. The Missouri Plateau and Drift Prairie rises above the Red River Valley, ranging between 200 to 2,000 feet above sea level. The prairie is filled with small valleys, lakes, and rolling hills. To the north of the Missouri Plateau are the Turtle Mountains. In the western part of the state, the Great Plains expand seemingly forever into the horizon. The plains also feature a portion of North America's Badlands, which are eroded and exposed buttes of clay and stone that form unique land formations that seem to belong in the American Southwest.

The petrified forest found in Theodore Roosevelt National Park is the third largest concentration of petrified wood in the United States.

Petrified Forest Trail
Difficulty 4
Hike this 10.2-mile loop trail in Theodore Roosevelt National Park near Watford City to see the ancient remains of the giant trees that once dominated this area. While there are only two sections of trail where petrified wood can be found, there are beautiful buttes and grasslands surrounding you the entire way.

White Butte Trail
Difficulty 2
Hike this 3.4-mile trail in Theodore Roosevelt National Park near Bowman to reach the highest point in North Dakota atop White Butte. You'll have to ascend 456 feet to reach the top of White Butte, which sits at 3,506 feet above sea level.

Turtle River Nature Trail
Difficulty 3
Hike this 5.6-mile trail in Turtle River State Park near Arvilla to walk through the forested banks of the winding Turtle River.

Bison Plant Trail
Difficulty 2
Hike this 2.3-mile trail in Minot Park District in Minot to explore the region around the Souris River. There are several side trails that go further into the park.

A photo of Caprock Coulee Trail with Caprock Coulee behind it.

Caprock Coulee Loop
Difficulty 2

Hike this 4.4-mile loop trail in Theodore Roosevelt National Park near Watford City to explore some of North Dakota's Badlands. Explore the sedimentary buttes of the eroded Great Plains in the sunbaked landscape.

A view from the top of Buck Hill looking East over the rolling hills of North Dakota's Badlands.

Buck Hill
Difficulty 1

Hike this .4-mile trail in Theodore Roosevelt National Park near Bowman to take a short stroll to the top of Buck Hill.

A photo of Wind Canyon with the Little Missouri River bending through the landscape.

Wind Canyon Trail
Difficulty 1

Hike this .5-mile trail in Theodore Roosevelt National Park near Watford City to explore this shallow, pastured valley. At the end there are great views of the Little Missouri River and grasslands around you.

A pelican and turtle hanging out in the remote Harmon Lake.

Harmon Lake Trail
Difficulty 3

Hike this 8.3-mile trail near Mandan to explore the grasslands and hills surrounding the shores of Lake Mandan. You'll walk around the entirety of the lake over wetlands and pastures on the boardwalk and rocky trail.

A side view of the replica of General Custer's house. The original was abandoned and torn down after the Lakota gained victory in the Battle of Little Bighorn.

Fort Lincoln Loop Trail
Difficulty 2

Hike this 3.6-mile trail in Fort Abraham Lincoln State Park near Bismarck. The fort played a significant role in the Black Hills Wars waged by the United States against the Lakota. The fort that stands today is the second location of the fort after the first was abandoned after Custer's 1891 defeat.

Sunrise over the Sheyenne River near Mineral Springs Trail.

Mineral Springs Trail
Difficulty 3

Hike 4.3-mile trail near Fort Ransom near the Sheyenne River to explore the hills and prairies of North Dakota's Red River Valley.

Ohio

Ohio is the thirty-fourth largest state in the United States and is the seventh most populous state with 11.8 million people living there. The state has several distinct topographical regions including the Appalachian and Allegheny Plateaus in the east, the Central Lowlands in the west, and the Lake Huron-Erie Plain in the north. The Appalachian Plateau in the eastern part of the state creates a rugged landscape of rolling hills, deep river valleys, and lush forests. The western portion of the state is filled with fertile low-lying plains that are dotted with wetlands and forests. The Great Black Swamp in northwestern Ohio is the remaining vestige of ancient wetlands left behind after the last glaciation. Because of Ohio's central location between the Northeast and the Midwest, Ohio has been a transportation and manufacturing hub for much of its statehood. It is within a day's drive of nearly seventy percent of the nation's population. Cleveland is the largest city along Lake Erie, and the state's northern border almost entirely consists of Lake Erie shoreline. Within the state, there are several important waterways including the Ohio, Cuyahoga, and Miami Rivers.

A sand covered trail from the eroded sandstone above in Cuyahoga Valley National Park.

Ledges Trail
Difficulty 2
Hike this 2.3-mile trail in Cuyahoga Valley National Park near Peninsula to walk along the moss covered ledges in this beautiful national park. This is a loop trail that will take you along the bottom of the ledges and then back around along the top of the ledges.

As you travel through Brandywine Gorge, you'll come across the magnificent Brandywine Falls.

Brandywine Gorge Trail
Difficulty 1
Hike this 1.4-mile loop trail in Cuyahoga Valley National Park to follow along Brandywine Creek through the creek's deep gorge. Go clockwise on the trail and you will go down first and then up on your way back, or follow along the upper side first by going counterclockwise and then down through the gorge on your way back.

Christmas Rocks Trail
Difficulty 3
Hike this 4.5-mile trail in Christmas Rocks Nature Preserve near Amanda to see Jacob's Ladder and Christmas Rocks. Jacob's Ladder is a rocky overlook that peers over Arney Run, while Christmas Rocks is an even higher overlook at the end of Jacob's Ladder.

Bender Mountain Loop Trail
Difficulty 3
Hike this 2.3-mile trail in Bender Mountain Nature Preserve up the rocky trail to the top of Bender Mountain. At the top, you'll have great views of the Ohio River.

A photo of the Upper Falls at Old Man's Cave in Hocking Hills State Park.

Old Man's Cave via Buckeye Trail
Difficulty 4

Hike this 9.4-mile section of the Buckeye Trail in Hocking Hills State Park near South Bloomingville to explore two caves in the region, Old Man's Cave and Ash Cave. You'll be able to see the recess cave where the hermit Robert Rowe lived around the turn of the nineteenth century.

A natural spring next to a stone staircase in Glen Helen Nature Preserve.

Glen Helen Multi-Trail Loop
Difficulty 3

Hike this 4-mile trail in Glen Helen Nature Preserve near Yellow Springs to follow along the banks of Yellow Springs Creek. You meander through quaint forests, cross the creek several times, and gain views of Ohio's Cascades region.

Rock House is a huge recess cave and is the only true cave in Hocking Hills State Park. It is located nearly 150 feet up the cliffside along the trail and requires some scrambling to reach it.

Rock House Trail
Difficulty 1

Hike this .9-mile loop trail in Hocking Hills State Park near Rockbridge to explore the Rock House Cave nestled into the gorge's sedimentary stone.

A beautiful waterfall tumbling over the ridge of Ash Cave.

Ash Cave Trail
Difficulty 1

Hike this .5-mile trail in Hocking Hills State Park near Creola to see the wonderful overhanging Ash Cave. The trail is paved up until you get to the mouth of the cave where it is covered in sand from the eroded stone above.

A small waterfall tumbling in Brecksville Reservation.

Deer Lick Cave Trail
Difficulty 3

Hike this 4.2-mile trail in Brecksville Reservation near Brecksville to hike through this forest past a waterfall on Chippewa Creek. At the end of this loop trail is Deer Lick Cave.

Be sure to go to Horseshoe Falls after a rainstorm to see the water really cascade down the falls.

Horseshoe Falls Trail
Difficulty 2

Hike this 1.7-mile trail in Caesar Creek State Park near Waynesville to walk along Caesar Creek back to the falls. Once at the falls, you can cross over the suspension bridge and explore the rocky outcropping around the creek.

Oklahoma

Oklahoma is the twentieth largest state in the United States. The "OK" state is filled with several distinct regions featuring mountain ranges, forests, river valleys, plains, mesas, canyons, and buttes. In fact, Oklahoma is the most geographically diverse state in the United States, containing eleven distinct ecological regions, and it is only one of four states to contain more than ten. Some of these regions from west to east include the High Plains of the Oklahoma Panhandle, the Gypsum Hills, the Red Bed Plains, the Sandstone Hills, the Prairie Plains, and the Ozark Plateau. In general, the state descends in a slope from the higher-elevation western panhandle down to the low-lying Red River Valley in the southeast. The highest point in the state, Black Mesa, is located in the northwestern tip of the panhandle at 4,973 feet above sea level, while the state's lowest point is along the Red River at 289 feet above sea level. Oklahoma's four mountain ranges, the Arbuckle, Ouachita, Wichita, and Ozark Mountains, are all considered distinct ecological regions in the state as well. The state has forty-one state parks, two national forests and grasslands, and several other reserves for recreational adventurers to explore.

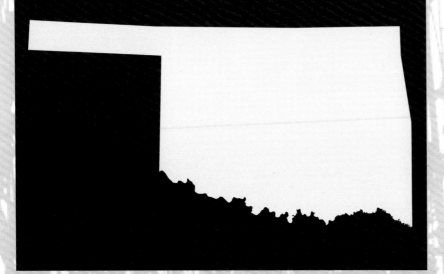

The Mountain Fork River flows from Ouachita Mountains in southeastern Oklahoma south to the Red River.

Charons Garden Wilderness is filled with large boulders of granite that you can scramble across in this rugged landscape.

Friends Trail Loop
Difficulty 2
Hike this 1.5-mile loop trail in Beavers Bend State Park near Broken Bow to walk along the ever-cascading Mountain Fork River. You'll descend a rocky trail as you work your way down to the banks of the river.

Elk Mountain Trail
Difficulty 3
Hike this 2.3-mile trail in Charons Garden Wilderness near Indiahoma from the banks of Headquarters Creek to the peak of Elk Mountain. You'll ascend just nearly 600 feet in the Wichita Mountains through the bouldery landscape.

Yellow Trail
Difficulty 3
Hike this 3.7-mile trail in Turkey Mountain Urban Wilderness in Tulsa to climb to the top of Turkey Mountain along the banks of the Arkansas River. Only ten minutes from downtown Tulsa, this park offers several great trails to explore the hilly regions of the Ozark Plateau.

Tree Trail
Difficulty 2
Hike this 1.2-mile trail in Beavers Bend State Park near Broken Bow to follow Beaver Creek and explore its lush floodplain.

A tiny waterfall in Roman Nose State Park. The park features three natural springs and a hilly landscape filled with gypsum bluffs.

Inspiration Point Loop
Difficulty 3

Hike this 5.8-mile loop in Roman Nose State Park near Watoga to explore the shores of Boecher and Watoga Lakes. Then follow along the banks of several creeks fed by natural springs. There are several creek crossings along the way.

The falls are beautiful at Natural Falls State Park, but no swimming is allowed.

Dripping Springs Trail
Difficulty 2

Hike this 1.1-mile trail in Natural Falls State Park near Colcord to follow the creek to the seventy-seven-foot waterfall. Along the way, you'll pass a natural spring and dramatic bluffs.

A photo from Bison Trail of French Lake with the Wichita Mountains behind it.

Bison Trail
Difficulty 3

Hike this 6.1-mile trail through Wichita Mountains National Wildlife Refuge near Indiahoma to walk through the rugged landscape of granite boulders. Follow the shoreline of French Lake and then along the gorge of West Cache Creek.

Black Mesa State Park is filled with beautiful rock formations and slender buttes.

Black Mesa Trail
Difficulty 4

Hike this 8.4-mile hike in Black Mesa State Park and Nature Reserve near Kenton in the far west side of Oklahoma's panhandle to the state's highest point. Black Mesa is 4,973 feet above sea level, and you'll see great views of the surrounding buttes and mesas on your way to the top.

A rainbow arching over the Ouachita Mountains and the Mountain Fork River in Beavers Bend State Park.

Skyline Trail
Difficulty 5

Hike this 9.5-mile loop trail in Beavers Bend State Park where you'll ascend nearly 1,600 feet into the Kimchi Mountains, a subrange of the Ouachita Mountains. There are several steep sections during the ascent and several watercrossings that may be difficult depending on water levels.

A view of Lake Lawtonka from the top of Mount Scott.

Mount Scott Overlook
Difficulty 5

Hike this 5.6-mile trail in Wichita Mountains National Wildlife Refuge near Medicine Park to ascend nearly 1,000 feet to the top of Mount Scott. At the top, you will have panoramic views of the entire Wichita Mountain region.

Oregon

Oregon is the ninth largest state in the United States and is one of the nation's most geographically diverse states. It has Pacific Ocean coastline, volcanoes, alpine mountains, high deserts, shrublands, and evergreen and mixed forests. It is home to one national park and several forests. The state's highest point, Mount Hood, is a potentially active stratovolcano that stands at 11,239 feet above sea level with several glaciers and ice fields surrounding its base. The state has eight distinct geographical ecosystems that give the state its unique terrain, including the Willamette Valley, the Oregon Coast, the Rogue Valley, the Cascade Range, the Klamath Mountains, the Columbia Plateau, the High Desert, and the Blue Mountains. The state has an average elevation of 3,000 feet above sea level and ranges from rainforests to true frontier desert. The state is home to several well-defined mountain peaks and possibly the nation's shortest river, the Roe River, which is only about 200 feet in length. The state has a very large number of animals and mammals that can be found in its borders, including moose, gray wolves, antelope, seals, sea lions, gray whales, killer whales, blue whales, sperm whales, lynxes, bobcats, cougars, elk, black bears, and foxes. With such diversity presented by the state's several landscapes, there is something for everyone to explore in Oregon.

A photo of North Falls along Ten Falls Trail in Silver Falls State Park.

A photo from under South Falls along Ten Falls Trail in Silver Falls State Park.

Trail of Ten Falls
Difficulty 4

Hike this 7.4-mile trail in Silver Falls State Park near Mehama as you ascend nearly 1,200 feet along the North Fork Silver Creek. Along the way you will walk through dense evergreen forest and pass, indeed, ten different waterfalls ranging from 27 to 178 feet tall.

Ramona Falls is a cascading wall-like waterfall that stands nearly 120 feet tall.

Ramona Falls Trail
Difficulty 4
Hike this 7.1-mile loop trail in Mount Hood Wilderness near Rhododendron to hike up to the falls around the base of Mount Hood. This trail has a gradual incline and a creek crossing at the beginning. There are sweeping views of the surrounding area around every turn.

The Tamolitch Blue Pool truly has blue waters that are fed by the McKenzie River, which emerges from a lava tube.

McKenzie River Trail
Difficulty 2

Hike this 2.6-mile trail in Willamette National Forest near Blue River to reach the shores of the Tamolitch Blue Pool along the McKenzie River. You'll start in a old-growth Douglas fir forest and then walk along a cliffside that you will eventually descend into the creek bed.

The summit of Angel's Rest is composed of andecite rock that was deposited by an ancient lava flow from Larch Mountain.

Angel's Rest
Difficulty 4

Hike this 4.5-mile hike in Shepperd's Dell State Natural Area near Corbett to ascend nearly 1,400 feet to the summit of Angel's Rest. You'll walk along a shaded and rocky trail up to panoramic views of the Columbia River Gorge. Rocky outcroppings, waterfalls, and deep forests await you on this trail.

At the top of Garfield Peak with a view of Crater Lake and Wizard Island in Crater Lake National Park.

Garfield Peak Trail
Difficulty 3
Hike this 3.6-mile trail in Crater Lake National Park near Crater Lake to ascend nearly 1,000 feet and follow the ridgeline of Garfield Peak around Crater Lake. You get sweeping views of the Cascade Mountains, Wizard Island, Mount Mazama, and many other stunning landforms.

Oregon's High Desert region provides outdoor enthusiasts several opportunities for great day hikes like this one in Smith Rock State Park.

Misery Ridge & River Trail
Difficulty 3
Hike this 3.5-mile loop trail in Smith Rock State Park near Terrebonne to walk the ridge-lined peninsula nestled between the bends of Crooked River. You'll scramble up steep rocks, walk narrow trails along steep drop offs, and cross a foot bridge to reach the views along Misery Ridge.

A photo of South Sister (left) and Broken Top (right). South Sister is the third tallest mountain in the state of Oregon.

South Sister Trail
Difficulty 5

Hike this 11.6-mile trail in Three Sisters Wilderness near Sisters to experience a hike so challenging you'll want to take a few days to complete it. You'll ascend nearly 5,000 feet on this trail to summit South Sister at nearly 10,000 feet above sea level. From the top you'll have views of Middle Sister and North Sister, as well as Three Fingered Jack, Mount Hood, and Broken Top.

God's Thumb via The Knoll
Difficulty 4

Hike this 4.3-mile trail in Siuslaw National Forest near Neotsu on the Oregon Coast. This famous basalt rock formation awaits you at the end of this trail after you ascend nearly 1,100 feet. From the top you will also see the Salmon River and Cascade Head.

The narrow trail leads out to God's Thumb in Siuslaw National Forest.

The Dry Creek Falls drops 74 feet over a basalt rock formation in Columbia River Gorge National Scenic Area.

Dry Creek Fall via Pacific Coast Trail
Difficulty 3

Hike this 4.4-mile section of Pacific Coast Trail in Columbia River Gorge National Scenic Area near Cascade Locks to come across the tremendous Dry Creek Falls. The pool at the bottom of the waterfall is perfect for a dip on hot days.

A view of Cape Falcon from Oswald West State Park.

Cape Falcon Trail
Difficulty 3

Hike this 4.6-mile trail in Oswald West State Park near Nehalem on the Pacific Coast to walk through the evergreen forests out to sweeping views of the coast. You'll only ascend about 600 feet through Sitka spruce forests.

Pennsylvania

Pennsylvania is the thirty-third largest state in the United States and the fifth most populous. It varies from low-lying coastal plains to the mountainous highlands of Appalachia. Pennsylvania's eastern side is a part of the Atlantic Coastal Plain and then rises in elevations toward the Piedmont Plateau. The Ridge and Valley region of the Appalachian Mountains and the Allegheny Plateau lie west of the Piedmont Plateau. The very western side of the state descends again in elevation as you approach the shores of Lake Erie. Pennsylvania is the only state of the original thirteen colonies that does not have coastline with the Atlantic Ocean, and its shoreline along Lake Erie is only 57 miles long. The state has several major rivers, including the Delaware, Susquehanna, Monongahela, Allegheny, and the Ohio Rivers. Pennsylvania's Ridge and Valley region of the Appalachian Mountains cuts through the state in an *S*-curve from southwest to northeast. This topography made much of the interior of the state difficult for exploration, and settlers and explorers relied on water gaps along the Susquehanna River to access the deep and lush valleys of central Pennsylvania. The Allegheny Plateau has similar ridge and valley formations but the valleys are much less deep than those found in Pennsylvanian Appalachia. Aside from the state's various regions, there are several cultural regions that one can explore, including the dense urban center of Philadelphia or the quaint countryside in the western Dutch Country.

One of the twenty-one waterfalls you'll see on the Ricketts Glen Falls Loop.

Ricketts Glen Falls Loop
Difficulty 5

Hike this 8-mile loop trail in Ricketts Glen State Park near Sweet Valley and ascend nearly 1,100 feet into the Appalachian Mountains. This is one of the most difficult and rewarding waterfall hikes on the East Coast. You'll walk Ganoga Glen and Glen Leigh to visit twenty-one waterfalls along Kitchen Creek.

Pulpit Rock overlooking the Appalachian Valley below.

Pulpit Rock & Pinnacle Loop
Difficulty 5

Hike this 9-mile loop trail near Hamburg to ascend nearly 1,200 feet to Pinnacle and Pulpit Rock overlook. The trail can be very steep and rocky, but the views of the Susquehanna River are beautiful.

Kelly's Run Loop Trail
Difficulty 3

Hike this 3.7-mile trail to the banks of the Susquenhanna River in Holtwood Recreation Park in Holtwood. There is a waterfall along Kelly's Run, and the trail can be awfully steep in sections.

Hawk Falls along Hawk Run in Hickory Run State Park. The park offers 44 miles of trail for hiking.

Hawk Falls Trail
Difficulty 1
Hike this 1-mile trail in Hickory Run State Park near Albrightsville to walk along Hawk Run to the falls at the end. This trail is short and sweet but can be very muddy certain times of the year.

The summit of Hawk Mountain is incredibly bouldery, so it's best to wear shoes with good ankle support.

Hawk Mountain Loop
Difficulty 4
Hike this 5.4-mile loop trail in the Hawk Mountain Sanctuary near Hamburg and ascend nearly 1,000 feet to the top of Hawk Mountain. You'll scramble, rock hop, and walk up large slabs of rock to make your way to the summit.

Valley Forge National Historical Park is filled with several historical markers from the Revolutionary War, like the National Memorial Arch seen here.

Mount Misery, Chapel Path & Mount Joy Trail
Difficulty 3
Hike this 7.5-mile trail in Valley Forge National Historical Park near Malvern. The trail is paved or gravel at various sections, and you'll walk past the ruins of an old church along the Schuylkill River.

Laurel Run along Audubon Loop Trail in Seven Tubs Recreation Area.

Audubon Loop Trail
Difficulty 2
Hike this 2-mile trail in Seven Tubs Recreation Area near Wilkes-Barre down the gorge along Laurel Run and Wheelbarrow Run. Although you'll ascend 219 feet, the trail consists of six-percent grades coming up and down from the creek.

The steps along Thousand Steps Trail are not very uniform and present a difficult challenge for many hikers.

Thousand Steps
Difficulty 4
Walk up several hundred steps in State Game Land Number 112 near Mill Creek to gain views of the Juniata River. You'll start on the banks of the Juniata River and work your way seemingly straight up the side of Jacks Mountain.

A photo of the Delaware Water Gap from Pennsylvania's Cliff Trail Loop.

Hackers Falls & Cliff Trail Loop
Difficulty 3
Hike this 3.7-mile trail in Delaware Water Gap National Recreation Area near Milford. You'll walk along the cliff line looking over the Delaware River and then back and around to a small pond before you return to the trail head.

In recent years, the Glen Onoko Falls have faced closures from severe erosion after heavy rains.

Lehigh Gorge Overlook Trail
Difficulty 3
Hike this 3.2-mile trail in the Lehigh Gorge Start Park near Weatherly to walk on the rim of Lehigh Gorge to peak down to see the Lehigh River below. Follow the stairs down into the gorge to see Glen Onoko Falls. There is also a platform along the ridge overlooking the gorge.

Rhode Island

Rhode Island is the smallest state in the United States. The state's major geographic feature is the Narragansett Bay with nearly 384-miles of shoreline. The bay contains nearly thirty islands, including Aquidneck Island, the largest island in the bay which is home to the cities of Portsmouth, Middletown, and Newport. Block Island lies twelve miles south off the coast of the state and sits in the waters between the Atlantic Ocean and the Block Island Sound. Much of the state is a flat coastal plain and there are no mountains in the state. The eastern portion of Rhode Island is a part of the coastal low-lands surrounding Narragansett Bay, while western Rhode Island is a part of the New England Uplands. The state's average elevation is only 200 feet above sea level, while the state's highest point is Jerimoth Hill at 812 feet above sea level. The state rock, Cumberlandite, is very rare and can only be found in the state at two known deposit points near the town of Cumberland. The rock is composed of iron ore and has been mined extensively due to its ferrous characteristics. Rhode Island may be small but there are plenty of places to explore in this New England setting.

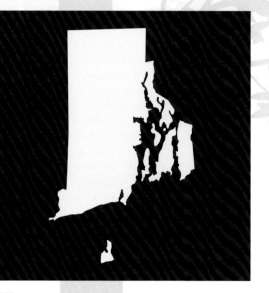

A photo of Bailey's Beach and Cliff Walk Trail. Bailey's Beach is a private beach whose membership has been criticized due to its lack of diversity.

Cliff Walk
Difficulty 1
Hike or walk this 7-mile trail in the town of Newport at the very southern end of Aquidneck Island to see some of the area's extravagant mansions from an age long gone. You'll walk the shoreline of the Atlantic Coast to Bailey's Beach.

A photo of lush pine stands lining the shores of Tarbox Pond in Big River State Management Area.

Carr's Pond & Tarbox Pond Trail
Difficulty 3
Hike this 4-mile trail in Big River State Management Area near Coventry to walk the entirety of Carr's Pond and then along some of Tarbox Pond. There are several spur trails branching from this trail that you can use to explore more of the park.

A photo of Stepstone Falls tumbling under the autumnal foliage.

Ben Utter Trail
Difficulty 2
Hike this 2.7-mile trail in Arcadia State Management Area near West Greenwich to walk along Baker Brook to Stepstone Falls. There are several other trails that spur from this trail that you can use to explore more of this area.

Fisherville Brook Wildlife Refuge Trail
Difficulty 3
Hike this 3.3-mile trail in Fisherville Brook Wildlife Refuge near Exeter to walk along Fisherville Brook.

Cumberland Monastery Trail
Difficulty 2
Hike this 3.2-mile trail around the Cumberland Monastery near Cumberland to explore the grounds of a former Cistercian Monastery.

Long Pond Woods Trail
Difficulty 3
Hike this 4.5-mile trail in Rockville Management and Public Fishing Area near Hope Valley to walk the shores of Long and Ashville Ponds. The trail is very rocky and will involve several scrambles up rock slabs along the way.

A photo of Stillwater Reservoir in the Wolf Hill Forest Preserve.

World War II Memorial Loop
Difficulty 3

Hike this 4.4-mile loop trail in Wolf Hill Forest Preserve near Smithfield and walk along the Stillwater Reservoir. Along the way you'll see the World War II Memorial located at a bomber crash site, an abandoned Boy Scouts camp, the upper Narragansett Bay, a rock quarry, and a waterfall.

A view of Narragansett Bay from Bissel Island.

Rome Point Trail
Difficulty 2

Hike this 2.4-mile trail in John H. Chafee Nature Preserve near Saunderstown to enjoy the views of Narragansett Bay and Conanicut and Bissel Islands across the water. You'll walk out on a narrow peninsula, Rome Point, and find yourself calmed by the wonderful sights before you.

A view of the Olney Pond from the Lincoln Woods Trail.

Lincoln Woods Trail
Difficulty 3

Hike this 3.1-mile trail in Lincoln Woods State Park near Lincoln to explore the shore of Olney Pond. This trail is paved and has several spur trails branching from it that will lead you deeper into the woods.

The trail nearing the end of Sachuest Point looking back toward the Breakers in Newport.

Sachuest Point Natural Wildlife Refuge Trail
Difficulty 1

Hike this 2.4-mile trail in Sachuest Point National Wildlife Refuge near Newport on Aquidneck Island. This trail will take you out on a little peninsula, Sachuest Point, between the Sakonnet River and the Rhode Island Sound.

South Carolina

South Carolina is the fortieth largest state in the United States and is the twenty-third most populous. It has three distinct regions, including the Atlantic Coastal Plain in the east, the Piedmont Plateau in the central part of the state, and the Blue Mountains in the far northwest. The Atlantic Coastal Plain is composed of sedimentary stone with the soil mostly consisting of sand and clay. This area is home to the Carolina Sandhills, which is a 35-mile region of sand dunes and wind-blown sand sheets. The central Piedmont is filled with low-lying hills that were once used for agriculture, but due to changing factors have now been left to become reforested with loblolly pine. Moving west from the Piedmont, you ascend the Blue Mountain escarpment into the Blue Mountains of the Appalachian Range. These mountains continue into North Carolina and Georgia and are home to South Carolina's highest point, Sassafras Mountain, standing at 3,560 feet above sea level. The state is home to two national forests, several national historic sites, several national military sites, and several forts that all offer activities outdoor enthusiasts can enjoy.

A view of Table Rock Lookout from Table Rock Reservoir, the exact opposite view you would have taking the Table Rock Trail.

Here we see the upper and lower sections of Rainbow Falls. Combined, the falls create a hundred foot drop from the granite and amphibolite ledges.

Table Rock Trail
Difficulty 4
Hike this 6.9-mile trail in Table Rock State Park near Cleveland to ascend nearly 2,300 feet to Table Rock Lookout and see the rolling Blue Mountains and Table Rock Reservoir in the distance. You will scramble up large slabs of rock, climb uneven stairs, and take on steep inclines on this very difficult trail. There are several water sources along the trail for you to fill up on water.

Rainbow Falls Trail
Difficulty 4
Hike this 4.4-mile trail in Jones Gap State Park near Cleveland and ascend nearly 1,800 feet up several stairs to reach the falls. The beginning of the trail is relatively flat and easy, but be prepared for a seemingly relentless ascent once you begin the stairs.

A view of Raven Cliff Falls in Caesars Head State Park.

Raven Cliff Falls & Dismal Trail Loop
Difficulty 5
Hike this 8.8-mile trail in Caesars Head State Park near Cleveland and ascend nearly 2,200 feet into the Blue Mountains. There are rung ladders, rings installed into slabs of rock, a suspension bridge, steep inclines, switchbacks, and all sorts of challenges along the way before you get to the magnificent falls.

Yellow Branch Falls gently cascades fifty feet down the rock face, but it can become just a trickle if it there hasn't been much rain.

Yellow Branch Falls Trail
Difficulty 2
Hike this 3-mile trail in Stumphouse Mountain Bike Park near Walhalla to enjoy this quiet walk through the hardwoods of South Carolina. You'll cross several streams before you reach the waterfall at the end of the trail.

A view of Keowee Lake from Raven Rock Loop Trail in Keowee-Toxaway State Park.

Raven Rock Loop Trail
Difficulty 3
Hike this 4.2-mile trail in Keowee-Toxaway State Park near Sunset to cross over Poe Creek along a natural granite bridge and climb up rocky outcroppings. You'll walk along the shores of Lake Keowee and through hardwood forests in deep valleys and along ridgelines before you loop back to the trailhead.

A photo of the verdant banks of Falls Creek.

Falls Creek Waterfall Trail
Difficulty 3
Hike this 2.1-mile trail near Slater-Marietta to climb up along Falls Creek to see several waterfalls. You'll start with a bit of an ascent, but the trail flattens out as you near the watefall. If you cross the base of the waterfall, there is a great picnic area on the other side.

A photo of North Lake in Paris Mountain State Park with the colors of fall almost in full effect.

Sulphur Springs Trail
Difficulty 3

Hike this 4.5-mile trail in the Paris Mountain State Park near Greenville to meander into the forest to see rock formations, brambles of rhododendron, a small lake, and several small creeks. It is recommended that you follow the loop clockwise because that will give you the best views along the way.

The Boardwalk Loop Trail keeps you out of the mud in the wetlands surrounding Congaree River.

Boardwalk Loop Trail
Difficulty 2

Hike this 2-mile trail in Congaree National Park near Gadsden through old-growth forests on a boardwalk six-feet above the forest floor. You'll explore the wetlands that surround the Congaree River.

Here we see Carrick Falls along Carrick Creek. There are several trails in Table Rock State Park that will take you along the beautiful banks of several beautiful creeks.

Carrick Creek Loop
Difficulty 2
Hike this 1.9-mile trail in Table Rock State Park near Pickens to follow along Carrick and Green Creeks as they tumble through the hardwood forests of the Blue Mountains. This trail is good for people of all abilities and ages, and there is fun to be had by all.

Probably one of the most beautiful waterfalls in the state, Lee Falls drops seventy-five feet in this shady ravine.

Lee Falls Trail
Difficulty 3
Hike this 2.9-mile out-and-back trail near Tamassee to cross through fields of wildflowers in the spring and then back into the woods before you reach the falls. There are several creek crossings along the way, so be prepared to get your feet wet. The falls at the end of the trail are beautiful.

South Dakota

South Dakota is the seventeenth largest state in the United States and is the fifth least populated state of all the states. South Dakota is composed of three different regions: eastern South Dakota, western South Dakota, and the Black Hills. The state is considered to be a part of the Midwest and is largely composed of the Great Plains, but western South Dakota seems more a part of the West recreationally, geographically, and economically. The Missouri River, the state's largest and longest river, bisects the state between east and west. Eastern South Dakota lies at a lower elevation than most of western South Dakota, with larger amounts of precipitation than western South Dakota or the Black Hills. The Coteau des Prairies, the Dissected Till Plains, and the James River Valley are all major geographic regions of the eastern part of the state. Western South Dakota is distinct from the eastern part in that it is much more arid and rugged. The region is home to the Great Plains and the famous Badlands of South Dakota, which features buttes and other formations from the eroded plains. Distinct from the rest of western South Dakota, the Black Hills are the state's third region with rugged granite mountains filled with cliff faces, hoodoos, and pine-filled canyons. The state's highest point, Black Elk Peak, rises 7,244 feet above sea level in the Black Hills and is the highest point in the United States east of the Rockies. South Dakota is home to several large Lakota reservations, whose populations compose a good percentage of the state's total population. South Dakota was home to several important events in the westward expansion of the United States and the Crazy Horse Memorial and Mount Rushmore pay homage to the state's complicated history.

The granite rocks of Custer State Park are truly a wonder and provide a beautiful backdrop along any trail you might hike in the park.

Sunday Gulch Trail
Difficulty 4
Hike this 3.9-mile trail in Custer State Park near Custer to climb nearly 800 feet along the shores of Sylvan Lake and then down into Sandy Gulch. The hike begins at the back end of Sylvan Lake down a steep trail into the gulch where you'll walk along a creek and pass awesome rock formations.

Custer State Park is extremely popular with rock climbers who love to climb the eroded granite cliff faces in the region.

Cathedral Spires Trail
Difficulty 3

Hike this 1.6-mile trail in Custer State Park near Custer to climb nearly 500 feet into the Black Hills to the base of the Needles, or Cathedral Spires, rock formation. This hike is great for kids looking to get out into the wilderness. Spend some time at the end of the trail and climb among the boulders and granite rocks.

The clay soil and sedimentary rocks of the Badlands have been eroded over several centuries. Badlands can be found on every continent in the world except Antarctica.

Notch Trail
Difficulty 2

Hike this 1.5-mile trail in Badlands National Park near Interior to experience the rugged terrain of the Badlands. You'll see the famous buttes and hoodoos of South Dakota's most famous park and climb a ladder up one of the trail's eroded hills. Be sure to bring lots of water because there is very little shade in the Badlands.

The last stretch of the hike to the top of Little Devils Tower can be extremely steep and will require a small amount of scrambling up rock slabs, which can be near impossible for dogs and small children.

Little Devils Tower Spur Trail
Difficulty 4

Hike this 3.6-mile trail in Custer State Park near Custer to do a bit of scrambling up rock faces to garner views of the surrounding Black Hills. Little Devils Tower is the diminutive look-alike to Wyoming's Devils Tower, but the views are still worth the effort.

A view of the fire lookout tower at the top of Black Elk Peak.

Black Elk Peak Loop
Difficulty 5

Hike this 7.1-mile trail in Custer State Park near Custer to ascend nearly 1,400 feet into the Black Hills to hike to the top of South Dakota's highest point. At the top of the 7,242 foot peak, you'll see panoramic views of the sacred lands of the Lakota people.

You will hike up 422 steps along Mount Rushmore and Presidential Trail Loop to the base of this presidential monument.

Mount Rushmore & Presidential Trail Loop
Difficulty 2
Hike this .9-mile trail in Mount Rushmore National Memorial near Keystone to climb to the rock pile that lies under the Mount Rushmore Monument. The pile was formed while carving the monument, and while you're there you will have unprecedented views of this famous monument.

If you get lucky, you just might come across an American bison while hiking in Custer State Park.

Lover's Leap Trail
Difficulty 3

Hike this 4.2-mile loop trail in Custer State Park near Custer to explore the gorges and then up to a granite ridgeline overlooking the state park. You'll walk along a beautiful creek and then up into the granite hills along a few steep inclines to get to the great lookout points.

The Castle Trail and Medicine Root Trail Loop is the longest trail in Badlands National Park and offers visitors the best way to explore the Badlands terrain.

Castle Trail & Medicine Root Trail Loop
Difficulty 5

Hike this 11-mile loop trail through the prairies and buttes of Badlands National Park near Interior to experience the rolling and stepped terrain of the region. This region of the Great Plains is truly magical and is filled with the serenity of an America of long ago.

A photo of The Door in Badlands National Park.

Door Trail
Difficulty 2

Hike this .8-mile trail in Badlands National Park near Interior to walk along a boardwalk to a break in the Badlands Walls. This break is called "The Door" and when you walk through this break you will be exposed to great views of the Badlands and its arid environment.

The Devil's Bathtub trail can require some technical skills at points to cross the creek, but the ascents and descents along the way are really not that steep for the moderately-experienced hiker.

Devil's Bathtub
Difficulty 2

Hike this 1.6-mile trail in Black Hills National Forest near Spearfish to walk along Spearfish Creek and its canyon down to the beautiful rock formations and eroded "tub." You will have to cross Spearfish Creek at points so be sure to be prepared for a water crossing.

Tennessee

Tennessee is the thirty-sixth largest state in the United States and is the sixteenth most populous. The state is split into three "Grand Divisions," East, Middle, and West, which are represented on the state's flag by the three stars featured in the center of the flag. Each region is geographically, culturally, and economically distinct from the others and many of these distinctions were defined by the Civil War. Western Tennessee was in support of secession from the U.S. because of its heavy reliance on slavery and plantation agriculture. The Middle and Eastern regions of the state did not support secession as Western Tennessee did due to the lack of agriculture supported in the region's rocky and mountainous terrain. Eastern Tennessee is dominated by the Appalachian Mountains with the Smoky Mountain Range and Ridge and Valley systems running through the region. The Cumberland Plateau separates the mountainous Eastern region from Tennessee's Middle region, which is characterized by table-topped plateaus around an elevation of 2,000 feet above sea level. The border along the Middle and West regions of Tennessee follows the dividing line between East Coast and Central Timezones. Western Tennessee is formed by the several low-lying river valleys, the Gulf Coastal Plain, and the Mississippi Alluvial Plain, which creates a region of fertile lands used for agriculture.

The Alum Cave Trail leading up to Alum Cave in Great Smoky Mountains National Park.

Alum Cave Trail
Difficulty 5
Hike this 10.9-mile trail in Great Smoky Mountains National Park near Gatlinburg to summit Mount LeConte and pass by Arch Rock and Alum Cave. You'll gain sweeping views along Duck Hawk Ridge and then continue to ascend the nearly 2,900 feet in elevation you'll gain along the trail.

Darwin's Revenge
Difficulty 2
Hike this 2-mile trail in Warrior's Path State Park near Blountville to walk to the banks of the South Fork Holston River. Most of the trail is covered in forest and there is very little elevation gain along the way, making this trail great for kids and dogs.

Spring Creek & Wilhoite Mill Loop
Difficulty 2
Hike this 2.4-mile trail in Henry Horton State Park near Chapel Hill to follow along Duck River and Spring Creek into the woods of Middle Tennessee. The trail can be muddy, so be sure to bring appropriate footwear.

Trotter Bluff Trail
Difficulty 1
Hike this .9-mile loop trail in Trotter Bluff Small Wild Area near Sevierville along the Tennessee River. This trail is perfect for a quick stroll through nature when you're walking the dog or when you want to get the kids out of the house.

Cherokee National Forest is home to several mammalian species including black bear, fox, bobcat, coyote, raccoon, woodchuck, and white-tailed deer.

Falls Branch Trail
Difficulty 2

Hike this 2.3-mile trail in Cherokee National Forest near Vonore in eastern Tennessee to the banks of Falls Branch. At the end of the trail, you will come to the tumbling Falls Branch Falls.

Piney Creek Falls tumbles ninety-five feet. There is an overlook along the trail that you can climb to the top for great views.

Piney Creek Falls
Difficulty 1

Hike this .7-mile trail in Fall Creek Falls State Park near Spencer to hike along Piney Creek and over a bridge to the beautiful falls at the end.

A photo of some of the waterfalls you will pass along the Emory Gap Trail in Frozen Head State Park.

Emory Gap Trail
Difficulty 2

Hike this 2.5-mile trail in Frozen Head State Park near Wartburg to walk along North Prong Flat Fork and Emory Gap Branch to see waterfalls and the peaks of the Smoky Mountains surrounding you.

A photo of the Bald River Gorge in Cherokee National Forest.

Bald River Trail
Difficulty 4

Hike this 8.8-mile trail in Cherokee National Forest near Tellico Plains to follow the Bald River on your way to Bald River Falls. The whole trail follows the banks of Bald River through forested landscapes.

Rainbow Falls cascades in a veil nearly eighty feet to the pool below in Great Smoky Mountains National Park.

Rainbow Falls Trail
Difficulty 5

Hike this 5.1-mile trail in Great Smoky Mountains National Park near Gatlinburg to ascend nearly 1,600 feet into the Appalachian wilderness. The trail starts with an ascent along Le Conte Creek and then to an overlook. From there, you'll cross several bridges and see several smaller waterfalls before you get to the thundering Rainbow Falls.

Chimney Tops is a double-capstone knob along the Sugarloaf Mountain range of the Smokies.

Chimney Tops Trail
Difficulty 4

Hike this 3.6-mile trail in Great Smoky Mountains National Park near Gatlinburg to ascend nearly 1,280 feet into the forested wilderness. At the top, you'll reach the summit of Chimney Tops, which sits at 4,725 feet above sea level, to gain views of the Smoky Mountains surrounding you.

Texas

Texas is the second largest state in the United States, and has the second largest population of all fifty states after California. With the state's massive size and central position, it is often considered to be a mix of the South, the Southwest, and Midwest. Although Texas is often thought of as mostly consisting of desert, only ten percent of the state's area is occupied by desert, which is found mostly in west Texas. The state is composed of four distinct regions, including the Gulf Coastal Plains, the Interior Lowlands, the Great Plains, and the Basin and Range Province; but due to the state's size, there are several smaller, distinct ecosystems located within these four larger regions. The northern panhandle is often compared to the Midwest due to the region's grasslands and prairies that are a part of the Great Plains. The Gulf Coastal Plain follows the state's 367 miles of Gulf of Mexico coastline and is filled with oak mottes, estuaries, grasslands, salt marshes, and sand dunes. The state's lowest point is here on the Gulf Coast at sea level, while the state's highest point is Guadalupe Peak at 8,749 feet above sea level in the Guadalupe Mountains of the state's western Basin and Range Province. This region is home to several mountain ranges and national parks including Amistad National Recreation Area, Guadalupe Mountains National Park, and Big Bend National Park. The Interior Lowlands are filled with rolling hills and dense pine-hardwood forests of oak, hickory, and gum trees. Texas occupies about seven percent of the total land and water area of the entire United States and cannot be easily classified due to its enormity. Texas truly is a state where everything is just a bit bigger. Whether it comes to expansive territory or population size, Texas is just downright big, and it offers plenty of big adventures for those looking to explore.

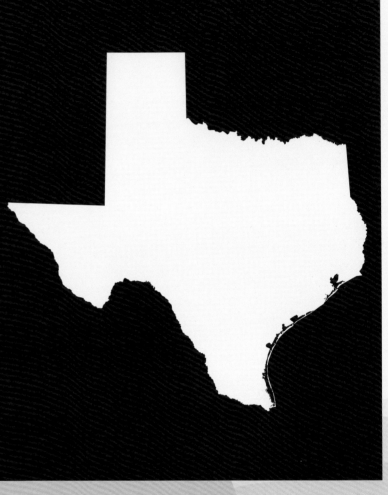

Lost Mine Trail
Difficulty 4

Hike this 4.8-mile trail in Big Bend National Park near the Mexican border to ascend nearly 1,100 feet in the Chisos Mountains. You'll pass through pine, juniper, and oak forest to mountain overlooks of Juniper Canyon, Casa Grande, and the Chisos basin.

A view of Juniper Canyon along the Lost Mine Trail in Big Bend National Park.

Eagle Mountain Lake Park Trail
Difficulty 3

Hike, walk, or run this 7-mile trail in Eagle Mountain Lake Park near Fort Worth to hike to the shores of Eagle Mountain Lake. You'll pass through shaded areas that open up to stunning views of the lake.

Crockett Gardens Falls Trail
Difficulty 3

Hike this 7.6-mile trail in Cedar Breaks Park near Georgetown to walk along the shores of Lake Georgetown to the park's wonderful gardens.

A view of the expansive Texas landscape from the top of Guadalupe Peak.

Barton Creek Greenbelt is a popular swimming destination for local Austinites.

Here we can see hikers taking in the views along the saddle of Lighthouse Peak.

The Window in the Chisos Mountains is a pour-out for rushing water during flash floods. It is extremely important to check weather conditions for rain before beginning the trail. Flash floods can be deadly.

Guadalupe Peak Trail
Difficulty 5

Hike this 8.4-mile trail in Guadalupe Mountains National Park near Salt Flat in western Texas to ascend nearly 2,900 feet to the summit of Guadalupe Peak, Texas' highest point. You'll pass through high deserts and high-altitude forests along switchbacks, but beware of the false summit because the real high point is another mile away.

Barton Creek Greenbelt Trail
Difficulty 1

Hike, walk, or run this 3.2-mile trail in Barton Creek Greenbelt near Austin to stroll along the banks of Barton Creek and see Twin Falls and Sculpture Falls. The falls might be dry depending on the season, but Barton Creek is always a great place for a dip and swim.

Lighthouse Trail
Difficulty 3

Hike this 5.8-mile trail in Palo Duro Canyon State Park near Canyon to summit Lighthouse Peak along the Caprock Escarpment of western Texas. You'll hike along and cross Little Sunday Creek and pass below Capitol Peak, Capitol Mesa, and Castle Peak before you ascend just 500 feet to Lighthouse Peak at 3,156 feet above sea level.

Window Trail
Difficulty 4

Hike this 5.2-mile trail in Big Bend National Park near the Mexican border to a beautiful overlook above the Chihuahuan Desert. You'll ascend nearly 1,000 feet through rolling hills at first and then between steep cliff sides before you climb through the pour-out.

A view of Enchanted Rock as you approach it along the trail in Enchanted Rock State Natural Area.

The Rio Grande serves as a natural border between Mexico and the United States.

Devil's Hall is a great place for rock climbing, but it's important to check the weather for rain before you go due to flash flooding.

Enchanted Rock Summit Trail
Difficulty 2

Hike this 1.3-mile trail in Enchanted Rock State Natural Area near Willow City to climb just nearly 500 feet to the panoramic views found atop Enchanted Rock. Enchanted Rock is an ancient pink-granite dome that has attracted people in Texas Hill Country for thousands of years.

Santa Elena Canyon Trail
Difficulty 2

Hike this 1.5-mile trail in Big Bend National Park near Terlingua to walk the banks of the Rio Grande with Mexico just on the other side. You'll cross the Terlingua Creek, ascend switchbacks, and then descend to the banks of Rio Grande surrounded by enormous limestone cliffs.

Devil's Hall Trail
Difficulty 2

Hike this 3.6-mile trail in Guadalupe Mountain National Park near Salt Flat in western Texas to enter into a tiny slot canyon carved into the creek bed. The trail starts in a mostly shaded area and then opens up as you walk along the rocky and bouldered creek bed. Devil's Hall provides nice cool shade between its towering walls.

Utah

Utah is the thirteenth largest state in the United States. The state's southeastern border along Arizona, Colorado, and New Mexico comprises the northwest corner of the Four Corners region of the Southwest. It is the thirtieth most populated state in the United States with most of its population centered around the Wasatch Front in north-central Utah and George County in southern Utah. The state contains a variety of geographic regions from high desert, pine-lined canyons and valleys, alpine peaks, white-water rivers, sand dunes, and salt flats. Utah's highest point is Kings Peak in the Uinta Mountains at 13,528 feet above sea level. The state lies at the intersection of the Great Basin in the west, the Rocky Mountains in the east, and the Colorado Plateau in the south. The Great Basin in western Utah, which stretches from Oregon through Nevada and into Utah, contains a large watershed system that does not drain into other major watersheds in the area. The area is arid with long-spanning basins disrupted by short mountain ranges. Much of southern Utah features beautiful sandstone rock formations, valleys, and canyons carved by the Colorado River and its tributaries through the Navajo and Kayenta sandstone of the Colorado Plateau. This area features several national and state parks and is known for its absolute natural beauty. Eastern Utah is composed of several sub-ranges of the Rocky Mountains including the Uinta and Wasatch Mountains. The Wasatch Front, which lies on the western edge of the Wasatch Mountains, contains nearly eighty percent of the state's population within 120 miles of development. Utah is truly a gem of a state, containing some of the most memorable outdoor recreation opportunities the nation has to offer.

Devils Garden Trail
Difficulty 4

Hike this 7.9-mile trail in Arches National Park near Thompson and ascend nearly 1,000 feet along the sandstone rock slabs to some of the area's most glorious arches. You'll see several arches like Double O Arch, Private Arch, Landscape Arch, Navajo Arch, Partition Arch, Tunnel Arch, and Pine Tree Arch. You'll also see the Dark Angel rock formation, which isn't an arch.

A photo of Landscape Arch in Arches National Park. Landscape Arch is the fifth longest arch in the world at 287 feet long. The top four longest arches in the world are found in China.

Dark Angel is a 150-foot sandstone tower just south of Double O Arch along Devil's Garden Trail.

Thor's Hammer, seen here, is probably the best known hoodoo in the park and was formed by differential weathering of the sandstone that eroded some portions faster than other portions.

Navajo Loop & Queen's Canyon Trail
Difficulty 3
Hike this 2.9-mile loop trail in Bryce Canyon National Park near Bryce to walk through the hoodoos, spires, and sandstone formations that make Bryce Canyon so scenic. You'll pass the rock formations Queen Victoria and Thor's Hammer and also gain exquisite views of the multicolored canyons in this high-desert terrain.

A view of Delicate Arch in the serene and often surreal Colorado Plateau of southern Utah's high-desert.

Delicate Arch Trail
Difficulty 3
Hike this 3.2-mile trail in Arches National Park near Moab to walk across giant slabs of sandstone to one of the nation's most famous natural arches. Follow along the rock cairns on the slickrock slabs and be sure to bring sunscreen and water because you will be exposed to the harsh desert elements along the way.

Twin Peaks Wilderness is home to several species of wildlife and sightings along the Lake Blanche Trail happen often.

Lake Blanche Trail
Difficulty 5

Hike this 6.8-mile trail in Twin Peaks Wilderness near Mounthaven in the Uinta-Wasatch-Cache National Forest to ascend nearly 2,800 feet to Lake Blanche, Lake Florence, and Lake Lillian. You'll start along the banks of Big Cottonwood Creek and then up into the wilderness with views of Sundial Peak off in the distance. Swimming is prohibited in the lakes because this area is a part of a protected watershed.

The Narrows are the narrowest section of Zion Canyon. Be sure to check weather conditions for rain because flash flooding in the canyon is common during the summer.

The Zion Narrows Riverside Walk
Difficulty 2

Hike or walk this 1.9-mile trail in Zion National Park near Springdale to walk along the banks of the Virgin River to one of the nation's narrowest slot canyons. The cliffside walls of the Narrows slot canyon tower above you as you walk close to water's edge. If you want to explore more, you can continue where the trail ends and go deeper into the canyon wading through waist-deep water.

A photo of Lower Bells Canyon Reservoir, where Bells Canyon Trail begins toward Lower Falls on Bells Canyon Creek.

Bells Canyon Trail
Difficulty 5

Hike this 4.6-mile trail in Uinta-Wasatch-Cache National Forest near Sandy up into Bell Canyon to Lower Falls. You'll hike along Bells Canyon Creek and ascend nearly 1,400 feet along a rocky trail to reach the quiet falls at the end of the trail.

A photo of Stewart Falls in Mount Timpanogos Wilderness.

Stewart Falls Trail
Difficulty 2

Hike this 3.4-mile trail in Mount Timpanogos Wilderness near Aspen Grove to hike through the forest along the eastside of Mount Timpanogos in the Wasatch Mountains. You'll follow this well marked trail to the 200-foot tall, double-tiered waterfall in Provo Canyon.

A photo of Mount Olympus in the springtime. Be sure to check weather conditions for avalanche risk before departing on the trail.

Mount Olympus Trail
Difficulty 5

Hike this 7.8-mile trail in Mount Olympus Wilderness near Cottonwood Heights to ascend nearly 4,100 feet to the summit of Mount Olympus, which stands at 8,993 feet above sea level. You'll climb high into the Wasatch Mountains through avalanche-prone alpine territory to gain sweeping views of Salt Lake City and the surrounding area. Scrambling and rock climbing make the trail quite difficult after the saddle, and crampons are recommended.

Ladders are set up along the Kanarra Creek Canyon Trail to ascend up the creek. Be sure to check weather conditions for rain in the area because flash flooding is a risk when entering slot canyons such as this.

Kanarra Creek Canyon Trail
Difficulty 4

Hike this 6-mile trail in Spring Creek Canyon Wilderness Study Area near Kanarraville to ascend nearly 1,000 feet along Kanarra Creek. You'll rock hop over the creek's waters, walk through the slot canyons, and climb up ladders over boulders to explore this magical landscape.

The drops along Angels Landing Trail can be very steep, but the steeper the drop-offs, the better the views.

Angels Landing Trail
Difficulty 4

Hike this 4.4-mile trail in Zion National Park near Springdale to ascend nearly 1,600 feet up through narrow canyons and along steep drop-offs to one of the park's best views of Zion Canyon. You'll start by crossing the Virgin River and then through Refrigerator Canyon into a set of twenty-one switchbacks called Walter's Wiggles. Continue from Scout's Landing along a narrow path next to Angels Landing, which provides views of Zion Canyon from 1,500 feet above.

Vermont

Vermont is the forty-fifth largest state in the United States and is the second least populated state. Montpelier is the least populated capital city in the U.S., and Burlington, Vermont's largest city, is the least populated largest city of any state. It is the only state in New England that does not share a coastline with the Atlantic Ocean. It may seem exceptional in all that it lacks, but Vermont contains large spans of wilderness that present several glorious outdoor opportunities. Vermont is fairly mountainous with the Green Mountains running the north-south span of the state just west of center. The Green Mountains contain several year-round alpine peaks, including the state's highest point, Mount Mansfield at 4,395 feet above sea level, Killington Peak at 4,229 feet, and Camel's Hump at 4,083 feet. The northwest border of the state runs along the shores of Lake Champlain, the United States' sixth largest body of water. Champlain Valley stretches soutward from the shores of Lake Champlain before it ascends into the Taconic Mountains of southwest Vermont. Vermont's eastern border runs along the Connecticut River, which forms a lush river valley along Vermont's eastern Green Mountains front. Nearly forty percent of Vermont is a part of the Connecticut River Watershed system. To the north, Vermont shares a border with the Canadian province of Quebec with fifteen official border crossing points. The state is still heavily forested with coastal oak forests lining the Connecticut River Valley, hardwood and conifer forests in the Green Mountains, and lowland Great Lakes forests in the area surrounding Lake Champlain.

A view of Camel's Hump from a distance. Rising to nearly 4,000 feet, Camel's Hump's alpine conditions can present challenging environments for many hikers.

Camel's Hump Trail
Difficulty 5
Hike this 6-mile trail in Camel's Hump State Park near Waterbury to ascend nearly 2,500 feet into the Green Mountains of Vermont. You'll make your way through lush pine forests to the top of Vermont's third highest peak for panoramic views of the surrounding wilderness.

One of the several rocky sections along Mount Mansfield Loop Trail. Be sure to leave early in the day to make the summit by early afternoon to avoid storms.

Mount Mansfield Loop Trail
Difficulty 5
Hike this 7.3-mile trail in Underhill State Park near Underhill to ascend nearly 2,800 feet to Vermont's highest peak. You will climb a rock wall and traverse a gorge early on the trail, and then climb the rock slab trail to Maple Ridge.

A view from the rocky outcroppings at the top of Killington Peak.

Bucklin Trail
Difficulty 5
Hike this 7.2-mile trail in Green Mountain National Forest near Mendon to hike to the summit of Killington Peak, Vermont's second highest mountain. You'll ascend nearly 2,400 feet in the Green Mountain wilderness. The trail starts with a gradual incline in lush pine forests and then into steeper alpine sections filled with rock slabs in need of scrambling.

Lye Brook Falls cascading over several layers of slippery rock. This area was once heavily logged and was filled with railroads and charcoals kilns, but it is now a wilderness area covered in second-growth forest.

Lye Brook Falls Trail
Difficulty 3
Hike this 4.4-mile trail in Green Mountain National Forest near Manchester Center to walk along the wooded banks of Lye Brook. You'll ascend just under 1,000 feet to reach one of Vermont's tallest waterfalls.

Hikers walking along the larger rock slabs at the top of Stowe Pinnacle.

Stowe Pinnacle Trail
Difficulty 4
Hike this 3.7-mile trail in CC Putnam State Forest near Stowe for a quick trip to the peak of Stowe Pinnacle at 2,600 feet above sea level. You'll ascend nearly 1,600 feet in under 2 miles but it never gets steep enough for you to need to scramble. This is a quick hike with exquisite views.

A snowy scene at Bingham Falls in Smuggler's Notch State Park.

Bingham Falls Trail
Difficulty 1
Hike this .5-mile trail in Smuggler's Notch State Park near Stowe to Bingham Falls along the West Branch Little River. This trail is great for all experience levels and takes you to a shady gorge where the water tumbles.

A view from Mount Philo overlooking Lake Champlain, the nation's sixth largest lake.

Mount Philo Western Loop
Difficulty 2
Hike this 1.9-mile loop trail in Mount Philo State Park near Charlotte to ascend nearly 500 feet for exquisite views of Lake Champlain. The trail can be steep but the ascent is quick and provides great overlooks for the effort.

Sterling Pond is a perfect mountain destination for swimming in the summer months, but the area can be closed in the winter due to weather.

Sterling Pond Trail
Difficulty 2
Hike this 2.3-mile trail in Smuggler's Notch State Park near Jeffersonville to the shores of Sterling Pond nestled in this narrow pass of the Green Mountains. You'll ascend just under 1,000 feet along a rocky, tree-lined trail through the quiet of Vermont's Green Mountain wilderness.

The Moss Glen Falls cascades over 100 feet along the Moss Glen Brook in CC Putnam State Forest.

Moss Glen Falls Trail
Difficulty 3
Hike this 5.2-mile trail in CC Putnam State Forest near Stowe to Moss Glen Falls in the dense hardwood, birch, and fir forests of the sub-alpine environment nestled at the base of Vermont's highest peaks. There is a bit of a climb to get to the best view of the falls, but the cascading falls are well worth the effort.

The shores of Dunmore Lake lined with beautiful fall foliage along the Falls of Lana Trail.

Falls of Lana Trail

Difficulty 4

Hike this 4-mile trail Moosalamoo National Recreation Area near Salisbury to ascend nearly 1,300 feet over the waters of Dunmore Lake. You'll see the Falls of Lana along Sucker Brook and then ascend to the rocky overlooks above the lake.

Virginia

Virginia is the thirty-fifth largest state in the United States and has the twelfth largest population. The largest city in the state is Virginia Beach but nearly thirty-six percent of the state's population can be found in the Baltimore-Washington metropolitan area. Virginia is split among two landforms separated by the Chesapeake Bay, with its major contiguous landmass sharing borders with Maryland, Washington, D.C., Kentucky, and West Virginia. Virginia's Eastern Shore is located on the Delmarva Peninsula across the Chesapeake Bay. On Virginia's western shore along the Chesapeake Bay there are several peninsulas, called the "fingers," that are formed by the Potomac, Rappahannock, York, and James Rivers flowing into the Chesapeake Bay. This eastern section of Virginia along the coast is called the Tidewater and is a part of the Atlantic Coastal Plain. Virginia then rises in elevation as you move west to the Piedmont Plateau. The Piedmont consists of igneous and sedimentary rocks that form the foothills of the Blue Ridge Mountains to the west. The Blue Ridge Mountains run from northeast to southwest through the state and is home to the state's highest point, Mount Rogers at nearly 5,700 feet above sea level. As you continue to move west, you move out of the Blue Ridge Mountains and into the Ridge and Valley region of the Appalachian Mountains. The Shenandoah Valley is called the Great Appalachian Valley everywhere else, but in Virginia it's the Shenandoah Valley. This region is composed of carbonate rock which allows for the easy formation of caves, and this section of Virginia features more than 4,000 limestone caves. Most are not open to the public, but there are several caves that offer tours like Luray Caverns and Skyline Caverns. Virginia is filled with a variety of landscapes you can explore from pristine shorelines along the Chesapeake Bay to the rugged mountains of Appalachia, so grab your hiking boots and find a trail to explore.

A beautiful view of the Shenandoah Valley from atop Old Rag Mountain.

Old Rag Mountain Loop
Difficulty 5
Hike this 9.5-mile hike in Shenandoah National Park near Etlan to ascend nearly 2,600 feet into the Blue Ridge Mountains to the peak of Old Rag Mountain. You'll ascend up rugged switchbacks that are still somewhat steep and scramble along large granite boulders.

Cascades Falls Trail
Difficulty 3
Hike this 3.8-mile trail in Jefferson National Forest near Pembroke to follow along Little Stony Creek to pass several smaller waterfalls before you reach the larger Cascades Falls. This trail can be crowded, but the hike is truly scenic.

Andy Layne Trail
Difficulty 5
Hike this 7.3-mile trail near Troutville to hike along Tinker Cliffs in the Appalachian Mountains. You'll cross the stream and begin a nearly 1,900 foot ascent to the Tinker Cliffs.

A view from the top of the Hawksbill Gap overlooking the Shenandoah Valley.

Hawksbill Loop
Difficulty 3

Hike this 2.7-mile trail in Shenandoah National Park near Syria to climb to the top of Hawksbills Summit for views of the Blue Ridge Mountains and Shenandoah Valley. You'll start at Hawksbill Gap and then pass several waterfalls before you begin a somewhat steep ascent to the summit.

A long-exposure photograph of Rose River Falls in Shenandoah National Park.

Rose River Trail
Difficulty 3

Hike this 3.8-mile trail in Shenandoah National Park near Syria to explore along the quiet and shady Rose River at the Fishers Gap Overlook along Skyline Drive. You will pass several waterfalls and the Rose River Falls, which fall nearly 67 feet.

Dragon's Tooth is a granite rock monolith on the top of Cove Mountain in Virginia's Appalachian Mountains.

Dragon's Tooth Trail
Difficulty 4

Hike this 4.5-mile trail in Jefferson National Forest near Catawba to ascend nearly 1,200 feet in the Appalachian Mountains. You'll pass through a shady forest along several rock formations and walls like McAfee Knob and Tinker Cliffs.

Crabtree Falls consists of five major cascades that fall nearly 1,200 feet.

Crabtree Falls Trail
Difficulty 4

Hike this 2.8-mile trail in George Washington and Jefferson National Forest near Tyro to wander through the mountainside wilderness along Crabtree Creek in the Appalachian Mountains. You'll ascend nearly 1,100 feet in little over a mile to the epic waterfalls at the trail's end.

A photo of the sunset from the summit of Bearfence Mountain.

Bearfence Mountain Trail
Difficulty 3

Hike this 1-mile trail in Shenandoah National Park near Hood to ascend only about 300 feet to the summit of Bearfence Mountain. The trail is extremely short, but it runs steeply up the mountainside to the summit of the mountain.

A photo of the boulderous summit of Sharp Top Mountain.

Sharp Top Trail
Difficulty 4

Hike this 3.3-mike trail in Jefferson National Forest near Thaxton to ascend nearly 1,200 feet to the top of Sharp Top Mountain, which sits at 3,829 feet above sea level. This trail goes straight up and then back down, so be prepared for a challenge.

One of the several waterfalls you'll see along Robinson River when you hike White Oak Canyon and Cedar Run Trail Loop in Shenandoah National Park.

White Oak Canyon & Cedar Run Trail Loop
Difficulty 5

Hike this 9-mile trail in Shenandoah National Park near Syria to ascend nearly 2,300 feet into the Blue Ridge Mountains to pass almost thirty waterfalls and humongous granite walls along Robinson River. You'll then begin your ascent to Hawksbill Gap at 3,360 feet above sea level along Skyline Drive and then back down along Cedar Run Creek.

Washington

Washington is the eighteenth largest state in the United States and is the thirteenth most populated with nearly 7.7 million people living within the state's borders. Much of the state's population is centered around the shores of the Puget Sound in the Seattle metropolitan area. The Puget Sound is a Pacific Ocean inlet with several deep bays and fjords and several islands. Western Washington starts in the Cascade Mountains and continues west to the Pacific Ocean shore, featuring deep rainforests, rocky shorelines, and several active volcanoes, including Mount Baker, Glacier Peak, Mount Rainier, Mount St. Helens, and Mount Adams. The summit of Mount Rainier is the highest point in the state at 14,411 feet above sea level. Mount Ranier is considered one of the most dangerous volcanoes in the Cascade Mountains due to its proximity to the city of Seattle. The Cascade Mountains are a part of the Pacific Ocean's Ring of Fire and are home to all of North America's volcanic eruptions in the last 200 years. West of the Puget Sound is the Olympic Peninsula, home to some of the nation's only rainforests and the Olympic Mountains. Eastern Washinton is much more arid than western Washington becasue of the rain shadow created by the Cascade Mountains. Eastern Washington features arid deserts and semi-arid steppe topography. Despite the region's arid climate, agriculture is extremely important for the region's economy and much of the population in this area is settled along bodies of water. Precipitation increases as you move further east away from the Cascade Mountains toward Washington's border with Idaho. Near Washington's northeastern border with Idaho are the Okanogan Highlands and Kettle River Range. In southeast Washington is the Palouse, a system of large grasslands that are vital to the state's production of wheat and legumes. No matter if you're visiting eastern or western Washington, there are plenty of majestic landscapes to explore.

Wallace Falls cutting through the pine forests in the Cascade Mountains.

Woody Trail
Difficulty 4

Hike this 5-mile trail in Wallace Falls State Park near Gold Bar to see the beautiful Wallace Falls along Wallace River. You'll ascend nearly 1,400 feet as you follow the river through the dense conifer forests of the Cascade Mountains.

The rolling foothills lining the base of Mount Rainier are home to truly beautiful landscapes that seem too good to be true.

Skyline Trail Loop
Difficulty 5
Hike this 6.2-mile trail in Mount Rainier National Park near Paradise Inn to ascend nearly 1,788 feet into the Cascade Mountains wilderness. You will hike along the southern base of Mount Rainier through dense forests to see views of the glaciers, waterfalls, and gorgeous landscapes.

Lake Twenty-Two nestled in the snowy mountain sides of Mount Pilchuck.

Lake Twenty-Two Trail
Difficulty 4
Hike this 6.8-mile trail in Mount Baker Snoqualmie National Forest near Granite Falls to ascend nearly 1,400 feet into the Cascade Mountains to the shores of an alpine lake. You'll pass through old-growth forest, cross over Twenty-Two Creek, and then climb up switchbacks to gain views of the surrounding mountains when you get to the lake.

A view of Rattlesnake Ridge from the shores of Rattlesnake Lake.

Rattlesnake Ledge Trail
Difficulty 4
Hike this 5.3-mile trail in Rattlesnake Mountain Scenic Area near North Bend to climb to the overlooks along Rattlesnake Ridge. You'll ascend nearly 1,400 feet to gain views of Rattlesnake Lake, Cedar Butte, and the surrounding Wenatchee National Forest.

A photo of Snow Lake surrounded by a snow-covered wilderness in Alpine Lakes Wilderness.

Snow Lake Trail
Difficulty 5
Hike this 6.7-mile trail in Alpine Lakes Wilderness near Snoqualmie Pass to hike high into the wilderness to the alpine Snow Lake. You'll ascend nearly 1,700 feet into the Cascade Mountains along South Fork Snoqualmie River to see waterfalls and then up rugged switchbacks to the shores of this beautiful lake.

A view from atop Mount Si with the Snoqualmie River Valley below.

Mount Si Trail

Difficulty 5

Hike this 7.5-mile trail in Mount Si Natural Resources Conservation Area near North Bend to ascend nearly 3,300 feet into alpine territory. This daunting hike is nearly all uphill with few flat areas to catch your breath. You'll be surrounded by lush forest for the first few miles before you break through the treeline. The higher elevations provide stunning views of the Snoqualmie River Valley.

A hiker along the shores of Lake Serene.

Bridal Veil Falls & Lake Serene Trail
Difficulty 5
Hike this 7.6-mile trail in Mount Baker Snoqualmie National Forest near Gold Bar into the Cascade Mountains to pass the beautiful Bridal Veil Falls and then walk to the shores of Serene Lake. You'll ascend 2,600 feet along stone steps and switchbacks to the ridge lined lake. Take a load off at Lunch Rock.

Colchuck Lake has emerald waters and is surrounded by the tremendous peaks of the Cascade Mountains.

Stuart Lake Trail
Difficulty 5
Hike this 9-mile trail in Alpine Lakes Wilderness near Leavenworth to Colchuck Lake nestled in the high mountains of the Cascades. You'll ascend nearly 2,200 feet on switchbacks after you cross the bridge over Mountaineer Creek. You'll see Dragontail and Colchuck Peak rising high above the water on the other side of the lake.

A view from the rocky summit of Mount Storm King looking over Crescent Lake.

Mount Storm King
Difficulty 5
Hike this 5.3-mile trail in Olympic National Park near Port Angeles on the Olympic Peninsula to gain scenic views of Crescent Lake from atop Mount Storm King. You'll ascend nearly 2,000 feet into the Olympic National Forest along switchbacks to reach this epic summit.

A photo of the fire lookout station on top of Tolmie Peak with Mount Rainier in the distance.

Tolmie Peak Trail
Difficulty 5
Hike this 5.6-mile trail in Mount Rainier National Park near Carbonado to ascend nearly 1,500 feet to the summit of Tolmie Peak. The trail ends at Tolmie Peak Fire Lookout where you garner unobstructed views of Mount Rainier just across the way.

West Virginia

West Virginia is the forty-first largest state in the United States and is the fortieth most populous. Known as the Mountain State, this state has historical ties to logging, mining, and several political and labor movements. The state is the only state to have formed after seceding from the confederate state of Virginia, and is only one of two states, along with Nevada, to achieve statehood during the Civil War. West Virginia lies entirely within the Appalachian Mountains and is commonly defined as Appalachia. The Allegheny Plateau of Appalachia composes much of the state's northeastern region and features Valley and Ridge topography as well as Spruce Knob, the state's highest point at 4,863 feet above sea level. Higher elevations in this region of the Monongahela National Forest create boreal woodlands of spruce trees and other conifers that are similar to colder climates found in Maine and Canada. The average elevation in the state is 1,500 feet above sea level, higher than any state east of the Mississippi. Western West Virginia is filled with the rolling hills of the Allegheny Plateau, which drop off steeply near the banks of West Virginia's western border along the Ohio and Big Sandy Rivers. Today the state is a haven for outdoor enthusiasts who do big things in the relatively low-lying mountains. The mountainous and rugged terrain provides opportunities for whitewater rafting, hiking, mountain biking, skiing, fishing rock climbing, and running.

A photo of Harpers Ferry across the Upper Potomac River from an overlook along the Maryland Heights Loop.

Maryland Heights Loop
Difficulty 4

Hike this 6.6-mile trail in Harpers Ferry National Historical Park near Harpers Ferry and ascend nearly 1,500 feet into the Valley and Ridge section of West Virginia's Appalachian Mountains. You'll hike along the banks of the Upper Potomac River, across the Goodloe Byron Memorial Footbridge, past the Civil War Campground, and then to Maryland Heights Peak at 1,500 feet above sea level.

Endless Wall Trail
Difficulty 3

Hike this 2.3-mile trail in New River Gorge National Park and Preserve near Lansing to walk along a seemingly endless cliffside overlooking the New River. You'll pass through lush forests along this rocky trail to reach several overlooks that provide stunning views of the river rushing 1,400 feet below you.

A view of New River from one of the overlooks along the Endless Wall Trail. New River has been following its present course for the last 65 million years, and some geologists consider it to be one of the oldest rivers in North America.

Loudoun Heights Trail
Difficulty 5

Hike this 6-mile trail in Harpers Ferry National Historical Park near Harpers Ferry to ascend nearly 1,400 feet to the Split Rock rock formation. You'll follow the path of the Loudoun Heights Skirmish of the Battle of Harpers Ferry during the Civil War and cross the Shenandoah River into the rugged wilderness.

Redman Run Trail
Difficulty 4

Hike this 3.7-mile trail in Spruce Knob-Seneca Rocks National Recreation Area near Cabins to ascend nearly 1,000 feet into the forested wilderness. The trail starts with an easy incline but becomes very steep near the end.

A view from Lions Head rock formation in the Dolly Sods Wilderness of the Allegheny Mountains.

Bear Rocks & Lions Head Loop
Difficulty 5

Hike this 19.6-mile trail in Dolly Sods Wilderness near Davis to spend multiple days hiking and backpacking through terrain above 3,000 feet in boreal woodlands. You'll hike along Red Creek, make creek crossings, ascend nearly 2,000 feet, and enjoy exquisite views of the surrounding area from Lions Head rock outcropping.

The rocky views from atop Spruce Knob, West Virginia's highest point.

Whispering Spruce Trail & Spruce Knob
Difficulty 1

Hike this .6-mile trail in Spruce Knob-Seneca Rocks National Recreation Area near Riverton to climb to the tallest point in West Virginia by only ascending 29 feet from the parking lot. This trail is incredibly easy and is suitable for all activity levels.

Beautiful views of the valley below on your way to the top of Chimney Top.

North Fork Mountain Trail
Difficulty 5

Hike this 5.3-mile trail in the Potomac Wildlife Management Area near Cabins to ascend an excruciating amount of elevation in just a few miles. You'll climb nearly 2,000 feet in just over two and a half miles before you reach the scenic views atop Chimney Top peak.

West Virginia is home to some of the most stunning views in the United States. Here we see the jagged Seneca Rocks towering over the autumnal foliage.

Seneca Rocks Trail
Difficulty 3

Hike this 3.6-mile trail in Spruce Knob-Seneca Rocks National Recreation Area near Seneca Rocks to ascend nearly 900 feet to overlooks of the Potomac River. Along the way there are plenty of large rock faces, cliffsides, and formations that are popular for rock climbing.

A hike atop Big Schloss rock formation along Wolf Gap Trail.

Wolf Gap Trail
Difficulty 4

Hike this 4.3-mile trail in Wolf Gap Recreation Area near Lost City to walk right along the border between Virginia and West Virginia and ascend nearly 1,000 feet into the Appalachian Mountains. The mile or so is incredibly steep but the trail then follows along a ridgeline to Big Schloss rock formation.

A view of Blackwater Falls in Blackwater Falls State Park.

Blackwater Falls
Difficulty 1

Hike this .4-mile trail in Blackwater Falls State Park near Davis to see the beautiful falls along the Blackwater River. You'll walk along a boardwalk through the forested state park to the falls along the river.

Wisconsin

Wisconsin is the twenty-third largest state in the United States and is the twentieth most populous. The state is composed of five distinct regions, including Lake Superior Lowlands, Northern Highlands, Central Plains, Western Uplands, and Eastern Ridges and Lowlands. Northern Wisconsin is mostly dominated by the Northern Highlands, which is home to the Chequamegon-Nicolet National Forest, glacial lakes left over from the last glaciation, and the state's highest point, Timms Hill at 1,915 feet above sea level. Nestled in the extreme north around the shores of Lake Superior is the Lake Superior Lowlands which extend no further inland from the shore than twenty miles and is characterized as a gently sloping plain leaning toward the lake in the north. The Central Plains region is a band of sandy plains, sedimentary rock formations, and rich farmland. The Wisconsin River cuts through this area, creating several sandstone buttes and cliffs as well as the gorges of the Wisconsin Dells. The Eastern Ridges and Lowlands extends along Wisconsin's eastern shore with Lake Michigan and is home to some of the state's largest cities including Milwaukee, Kenosha, and Madison. The Western Uplands is a hilly region that is part of the Driftless Area, an area in Illinois, Wisconsin, Iowa, and Minnesota that wasn't covered by the last glaciation, that is home to several bluffs and exposed rock faces along the Mississippi River. Nearly fifty percent of the state is still covered in forest, and despite the cold, there is a large amount of beauty to be found in this Great Lakes state.

West Bluff & East Bluff Loop Trail
Difficulty 3

Hike this 4.7-mile trail in Devil's Lake State Park near Baraboo to walk around the entirety of Devil's Lake. You'll walk along the eastern and western bluffs that surround the lake's shoreline. There are several steep sections, but the views of the lake are worth it.

Devil's Lake from a bluff overlook in Wisconsin's Driftless Area.

Willow Falls & Nelson Farm Trail Loop
Difficulty 3

Hike this 6.1-mile loop trail in Willow River State Park near Hudson to see the falls tumbling down several cascades in the Willow River Gorge. You'll meander through the rolling hills surrounding the north and south sides of the Willow River.

Willow Falls tumbles down forty-five feet along Willow River just miles before the Willow River exits into the Mississippi River.

Peninsula State Park is a great place for snowshoeing and cross-country skiing in the winter, or swimming and sea kayaking in the summer.

Eagle Trail
Difficulty 2

Hike this 2-mile trail in Peninsula State Park near Ephraim in Wisconsin's esteemed Door Peninsula between Green Bay and Lake Michigan. You'll explore a rocky trail that leads to a bluff overlooking the beautiful Green Bay waters.

Parfrey's Glen Creek and its trail can fall victim to flooding every few years, and the trail can be closed at points depending on the damage.

Parfrey's Glen Trail
Difficulty 2

Hike this 1.7-mile trail in Parfrey's Glen State Natural Area near Merrimac to hike up Parfrey's Glen Creek from stone to stone. You'll follow along the creek as the glen gets deeper and deeper. Hiking along the stream can be difficult for some hikers.

Lion's Den Gorge Nature Preserve is one of Wisconsin's last and largest stretches of undeveloped shoreline along Lake Michigan.

Lion's Den Trail
Difficulty 2

Hike this 1.9-mile trail in Lion's Den Gorge Nature Preserve near Grafton along a bluff overlooking the sandy beaches of eastern Wisconsin's Lake Michigan shores. You'll experience the true splendor of Wisconsin along one of the world's largest lakes.

The caves just north of Meyer's Beach along the shores of Lake Superior.

Meyers Beach Sea Cave Trail
Difficulty 2

Hike this 4.6-mile trail in Apostle Islands National Lakeshore near Bayfield along the far northern Lake Superior shore of Wisconsin to see beautiful sandstone coves. You'll look down upon the caves in the summer on the hike, but be sure to rent a kayak to approach the caves by water too.

A photo of Devil's Doorway overlooking Devil's Lake in the Driftless Area of Wisconsin.

Devil's Doorway Loop
Difficulty 2

Hike this 1.9-mile trail in Devil's Lake State Park near Baraboo to climb up the lake's eastern bluff to this beautiful rock formation. The stony stairway leads you up about 500 feet through the forest to great overlooks of Devil's Lake through the precarious Devil's Doorway.

Ice Age Trail Near Monches
Difficulty 3

Hike this 3.7-mile section of Wisconsin's Ice Age Trail near Moches to follow along the beautiful Oconomowoc River. You'll walk through the hardwood forests of central Wisconsin and cross over lightly tumbling creeks.

Mallard Lake Trail
Difficulty 1

Hike this 1.4-mile trail in Whitnall Park near Franklin to walk around the entirety of Mallard Lake to the falls along Tess Corners Creek.

Levis/Trow Mounds Trail
Difficulty 4

Hike this 5.5-mile trail in Levis-Trow Mound Recreation Area near Neillsville to hike through gorges around the mounds and through dense forest. The recreation area is full of several winding trails that you can explore if you are looking for more of an adventure.

Wyoming

Wyoming is the tenth largest state in the United States and is the least populated state. It is also the least densely populated state in the contiguous United States. The Great Plains meet the Rocky Mountains in Wyoming, dividing mountainous western Wyoming from the High Plains of eastern Wyoming. Much of the state is a high-elevation plateau that is broken up by a number of mountain ranges and basins. The Northern Rockies extend into southwest Wyoming in a range called the Snowy Range, which has several peaks above 12,000 feet above sea level. North of the Snowy Range is the Teton Range, home of Grand Teton National Park and Wyoming's second tallest peak, Grand Teton. In south-central Wyoming are the isolated Wind River Mountains of the Northern Rockies, which are home to several peaks exceeding 13,000 feet, including the state's highest point, Gannett Peak at 13,804 feet above sea level. In north-central Wyoming we find the Bighorn Mountains, which are quite distinct from the rest of the Rockies. In between all of these enormous mountain ranges are a variety of unique ecosystems found in the valleys and basins, including sand dunes, deserts, shrublands, and long grass-filled plains. Wyoming is extremely dry, with the entire state receiving only about ten inches of rain per year, but it is home to several natural springs and hot springs including the many geysers found in Yellowstone National Park. Wyoming is filled with wide open spaces and very few people, so we're sure you'll be able to find an adventure in the Equality State.

Old Faithful is a cone geyser that erupts predictably about every 45 minutes to two hours. When it erupts, somewhere between 3,500 and 8,000 gallons of boiling water are shot about 145 feet into the air. Old Faithful is so predictable because it is not connected to any other water features in the Upper Geyser Basin.

Geyser Basin & Old Faithful Observation Point
Difficulty 2

Hike this 3.9-mile trail in Yellowstone National Park near Moran to see several natural hot springs and geysers in the Upper Geyser Basin, including the famous Old Faithful geyser. This trail is accessible for people of all ability, but the boardwalk can be slippery when wet or cold.

Hiking in Cascade Canyon provides an opportunity to see all types of wildlife like moose, black and brown bear, and elk. Be sure to bring bear spray.

Cascade Canyon Trail
Difficulty 5

Hike this 9-mile trail in Grand Teton National Park near Jackson to walk through Cascade Canyon to the base of the Cathedral Group of Teton Peaks. You'll start along the shores of Jenny Lake and then ascend nearly 1,100 feet along Cascade Creek to Cascade Falls, Inspiration Point, and then to the base of the Tetons.

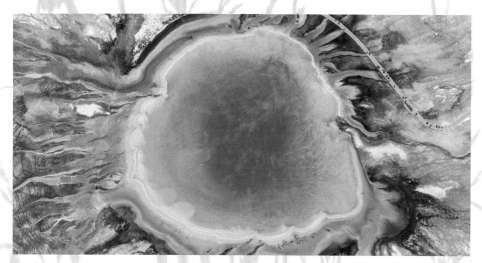

Seen from above the Grand Prismatic Hot Spring looks like the surface of another planet.

Grand Prismatic Hot Spring
Difficulty 1
Hike this 1.6-mile trail in Yellowstone National Park near Moran to see the largest hot spring in the United States in the famous Midway Geyser Basin. You'll walk along the boardwalk trailing between several hot springs filled with colorful microscopic life.

The waters of Lake Taggart are fed by the snowmelt from Avalanche Canyon, and its waters are still considered to be pristine and barely disrupted by air or water pollution.

Taggart Lake Loop
Difficulty 2
Hike this 3.8-mile trail in Grand Teton National Park near Jackson to loop around the shores of Taggart Lake. Along the way you'll enjoy great views of the lake as well as the surrounding Teton Range towering above you.

Curt Gowdy State Park is an awesome place to climb around and go bouldering for the day. The park provides several miles of trail for hikers to explore.

Crow Creek Trail
Difficulty 3
Hike this 3.6-mile trail in Curt Gowdy State Park near Cheyenne to follow Crow Creek from the shores of Granite Spring Reservoir to Hidden Falls. You'll have to climb a few boulders and wade through some water at the end of the trail to actually see the falls, which truly are hidden.

A view from the summit of Table Mountain with Middle Teton in the distance.

Table Mountain Trail
Difficulty 5
Hike this 10.7-mile trail in Jedediah Smith Wilderness near Alta to ascend an incredible 4,100 feet into the Teton Range to the peak of Table Mountain. You'll be high above sea-level at 11,064 when you reach the peak, but be sure to leave early to make it to the top and back before afternoon. This hike is no joke.

Climbing up to Darby Wind Cave can be hard and slippery, and exploring the cave itself can be even more difficult due to the steep dropoffs and deep waters.

Darby Canyon Wind Cave Trail
Difficulty 5

Hike this 6.3-mile trail in Caribou-Targhee National Forest near Alta to hike through the forested canyon to the large cave at the end. You'll cross over Darby Creek, pass a waterfall, and climb up and out of the canyon before you reach the huge cave. If you want to explore the cave, it is recommended to bring climbing gear.

Devils Tower was formed by the erosion of sedimentary stone that surrounded the igneous rock formation present today. It will continue to get taller as erosive forces continue to wash away the stone around it.

Devils Tower Trail
Difficulty 2

Hike this 1.7-mile trail in Devils Tower National Monument near Devils Tower to walk around the entirety of the rock anomaly rising up from the high plains. This place is great for rock climbing and bouldering, and if you want to get a closer look, go climb through the boulder field above the tree line to get up close to the tower.

Tongue River Canyon is a beautiful and serene canyon to enjoy a hike along with its towering walls of limestone and relatively flat and smooth trail.

Tongue River Canyon
Difficulty 3

Hike this 4.7-mile trail in Bighorn National Forest near Buffalo to travel into the canyon along Tongue River and then out of the canyon to the prairie above. There is a beautiful pool of water fed by Tongue River with a waterfall that you can rest at before you start making your return trip.

Porcupine Falls tumbles nearly 100 feet into the pool below.

Porcupine Falls Trail
Difficulty 2

Hike this .8-mile trail in Bighorn National Forest near Buffalo to the falls at the bottom of the trail. From the parking lot, you start your descent down to the falls along stairs, but be cautious because the trail gets a bit more steep and dangerous when the stairs end.